Allan Shepard

Ancient Rituals
Celebration of the Cycles of Celtic Spirituality

Original Title: *Rituais Antigos - Celebração dos Ciclos da Espiritualidade Celta*

Copyright © 2025, published by Luiz Antonio dos Santos ME. This book is a non-fiction work that explores practices and concepts within the realm of Celtic spirituality. Through a comprehensive approach, the author provides practical tools for reconnecting with ancient rituals, nature's cycles, and spiritual wisdom.

1st Edition
Production Team
Author: Allan Shepard
Editor: Luiz Santos
Cover Design: Studios Booklas / Thomas Whitmore
Consultant: Eleanor McAdams
Researchers: Patrick O'Connell, Fiona Hayes, Gregory Millman
Layout Design: Jasper Reynolds
Translation: Olivia Carter
Publication and Identification
Ancient Rituals: Celebration of the Cycles of Celtic Spirituality
Booklas Publishing, 2025
Categories: Spirituality / Mythology / Cultural Studies
DDC: 299.16 – **CDU:** 133.9
All rights reserved to:
Luiz Antonio dos Santos ME / Booklas Publishing
No part of this book may be reproduced, stored in a retrieval system, or transmitted in any form—electronic, mechanical, photocopying, recording, or otherwise—without prior written permission from the copyright holder.

Summary

Systematic Index 5
Prologue 11
Part I Foundations of Celtic Spirituality 13
Chapter 1 The Awakening 13
Chapter 2 Celtic Cosmovision 18
Chapter 3 Gods and Goddesses 24
Chapter 4 Sacred Spaces 30
Chapter 5 Ritualistic Preparation 36
Chapter 6 Celtic Symbols 42
Chapter 7 Ogham The Oracle 46
Chapter 8 Natural Magic 51
Part II: Rites of the Wheel of the Year 57
Chapter 9 Samhain Honoring the Ancestors 57
Chapter 10 Yule The Winter Solstice 63
Chapter 11 Imbolc The Purification 68
Chapter 12 Ostara The Spring Equinox 74
Chapter 13 Beltane The Sacred Fire 80
Chapter 14 Litha The Summer Solstice 85
Chapter 15 Lughnasadh The First Harvest 91
Chapter 16 Mabon The Autumn Equinox 97
Part III Rites of Passage and Celebrations 103
Chapter 17 Birth and Naming 103
Chapter 18 Initiation The Awakening 109
Chapter 19 Sacred Unions 115

Chapter 20 Healing Rites 119
Chapter 21 Celtic Divination 125
Chapter 22 Transition and Death 131
Chapter 23 The Awakening of the Celtic Soul 136
Chapter 24 Gratitude Rituals... 142
Part IV Deepening and Advanced Practice................................ 147
Chapter 25 Advanced Celtic Magic 147
Chapter 26 Shamanic Journeys 153
Chapter 27 The Druidic Tradition... 159
Chapter 28 The Path of the Bard... 165
Chapter 29 The Warrior's Path.. 171
Chapter 30 The Healing of the Earth 176
Chapter 31 Living Celtic Spirituality.. 182
Chapter 32 The Celtic Legacy 191
Epilogue 202

Systematic Index

Part I: Foundations of Celtic Spirituality

Chapter 1: The Awakening - Introduces the core principles of Celtic spirituality, emphasizing its connection to nature, the cycles of life, and the divine.

Chapter 2: Celtic Cosmovision - Explores the Celtic worldview, including the Wheel of the Year, the four elements, the three realms of existence, and the interconnectedness of all things.

Chapter 3: Gods and Goddesses - Delves into the vast and diverse Celtic pantheon, highlighting the main deities and their attributes, and offering guidance on how to connect with these ancestral energies.

Chapter 4: Sacred Spaces - Discusses the sacredness of nature in Celtic spirituality, identifying natural and constructed sacred spaces, and providing instructions on how to create a sacred space in your own home.

Chapter 5: Ritualistic Preparation - Details the steps involved in preparing for a Celtic ritual, including purification, protection, and the use of ritual tools and clothing.

Chapter 6: Celtic Symbols - Explores the rich symbolism present in Celtic culture, deciphering the meanings of the main symbols and explaining how to use them in spiritual practice.

Chapter 7: Ogham: The Oracle - Introduces Ogham, the ancient Celtic tree alphabet, explaining its history, structure, and use as a divination tool and magical system.

Chapter 8: Natural Magic - Presents the principles and practices of Celtic natural magic, emphasizing the connection with the elements, the use of herbs and crystals, and the importance of respect and reciprocity with nature.

Part II: Rites of the Wheel of the Year

Chapter 9: Samhain: Honoring the Ancestors - Guides the reader through the celebration of Samhain, the Celtic New Year, offering rituals and practices to connect with ancestors and honor the cycle of life, death, and rebirth.

Chapter 10: Yule: The Winter Solstice - Celebrates Yule, the winter solstice, with rituals and reflections on the rebirth of light, hope, and renewal, offering ways to connect with this ancestral energy.

Chapter 11: Imbolc: The Purification - Welcomes Imbolc, the festival of purification and inspiration, dedicated to the goddess Brigid, with rituals and practices to renew energies and prepare for the arrival of spring.

Chapter 12: Ostara: The Spring Equinox - Celebrates Ostara, the spring equinox, with rituals that honor the balance between light and darkness, the fertility of the earth, and the promise of growth and new beginnings.

Chapter 13: Beltane: The Sacred Fire - Ignites the Beltane fire, the festival of union, fertility, and the power of fire, with vibrant rituals and celebrations to connect with the energy of life in its fullness.

Chapter 14: Litha: The Summer Solstice - Honors Litha, the summer solstice, with rituals dedicated to the peak of the sun's power, abundance, gratitude, and the celebration of light and vitality.

Chapter 15: Lughnasadh: The First Harvest - Celebrates Lughnasadh, the first harvest festival, with rituals focused on gratitude for the generosity of the earth, recognition of sacrifice, and preparation for the future.

Chapter 16: Mabon: The Autumn Equinox - Concludes the cycle of the year with Mabon, the autumn equinox, with rituals focused on balance, gratitude for the harvest, and preparation for the challenges and opportunities of the new cycle.

Part III: Rites of Passage and Celebrations

Chapter 17: Birth and Naming - Describes the Celtic rituals associated with birth and the act of naming, highlighting the importance of protection, connection with the community, and the choice of a name full of meaning.

Chapter 18: Initiation: The Awakening - Explores the initiation rituals that marked the transition from childhood to adulthood in Celtic culture, emphasizing the importance of learning, challenges, and spiritual connection.

Chapter 19: Sacred Unions - Celebrates the Sacred Union, or marriage, in Celtic culture, highlighting its symbolism, rituals, and importance as a rite of passage that celebrates love, commitment, and the continuity of life.

Chapter 20: Healing Rites - Presents the healing rites practiced by the ancient Celts, combining knowledge of medicinal plants, connection with nature, and the invocation of the gods to restore balance and health.

Chapter 21: Celtic Divination - Delves into the practice of Celtic divination, exploring its methods, such as Ogham, the observation of nature, and the interpretation of dreams, to obtain guidance, make decisions, and connect with the spiritual world.

Chapter 22: Transition and Death - Addresses the Celtic view of death as a transition to the Otherworld, describing funeral rituals, mourning practices, and the importance of honoring ancestors.

Part IV: Deepening and Advanced Practice

Chapter 23: The Awakening of the Celtic Soul - Offers a guide to awakening the Celtic soul, integrating ancestral wisdom and Celtic spirituality into daily life through connection with nature, honoring ancestors, and developing intuition.

Chapter 24: Gratitude Rituals - Explores the power of gratitude in Celtic spirituality, presenting rituals, prayers, and practices to cultivate gratitude in everyday life and connect with abundance and divine blessings.

Chapter 25: Advanced Celtic Magic - Delves into the depths of Celtic magic, exploring more complex techniques, the connection with deities and spirits, and the ethical and responsible use of magical power.

Chapter 26: Shamanic Journeys - Introduces the practice of shamanic journeys in the Celtic context, guiding the reader through the preparation, induction of altered states of consciousness, exploration of spiritual realms, and integration of experiences.

Chapter 27: The Druidic Tradition - Explores the Druidic tradition, the history and role of Druids in Celtic society, their philosophy, practices, and the influence of Druidry in the modern world.

Chapter 28: The Path of the Bard - Delves into the role of the bard in Celtic culture, their functions as storytellers, educators, and spiritual guides, and offers guidance on how to connect with the bardic tradition today.

Chapter 29: The Warrior's Path - Discusses the values and principles of the Celtic warrior, emphasizing not only combat skills but also inner development, discipline, honor, and connection with the divine.

Chapter 30: The Healing of the Earth - Explores the Celtic view of the Earth as a sacred and living being, emphasizing the importance of caring for, honoring, and healing the planet, and offering practices and reflections to connect with this ancestral wisdom.

Chapter 31: Living Celtic Spirituality - Offers a practical guide to living Celtic spirituality in everyday life, integrating its principles and values through connection with nature, honoring ancestors, developing intuition, and expressing creativity.

Chapter 32: The Celtic Legacy - Reflects on the enduring legacy of Celtic culture in the modern world, its influence on art, literature, music, spirituality, and values, and discusses the importance of preserving and honoring this heritage.

Prologue

In a world where technology connects everything except the soul, humanity finds itself facing a void that modern religions no longer fill. This book delves into the roots of Celtic spirituality, where gods inhabited forests, rivers, and seasons, and the sacred was as vital as the air we breathe. The Celts did not venerate distant divinities—they lived in constant dialogue with the invisible, finding in storms, in harvests, and even in death the presence of a mystery that united all beings.

Modernity, by replacing altars with algorithms, has distanced us from this primal connection. But today, amidst the weariness of a progress that promised answers and delivered fragments, we turn our eyes to the past. In Celtic traditions, we rediscover a religiosity without dogmas, where the earth is not a resource, but a temple; where time is not linear, but cyclical; and where spirituality is not enclosed in temples, but pulses in every daily act.

This is not a book about history or mythology. It is a call to reconnection. A journey that reveals how, paradoxically, the same era that alienated us from the ancient gods now provides us with the tools to rescue them. In the voices of the druids, in the rhythms of the seasons, and in the wisdom of a people who saw the divine in everything, we find clues to heal the disconnection of the modern soul.

"Ancient Rituals" does not offer ready-made answers—it invites you to slow down, listen to the whisper of the leaves, and perhaps rediscover the spirituality that never ceased to exist: wild, free, and profoundly human.

Luiz Santos Editor

Part I Foundations of Celtic Spirituality

Chapter 1
The Awakening

Celtic spirituality is an invitation to return to our roots, to the ancestral wisdom that echoes in our souls. It is a call to reconnect with nature, with the cycles of life, and with the magic that permeates all things. More than a religion, Celtic spirituality is a way of life, a philosophy that teaches us to live in harmony with the world around us and with our own being.

Celtic spirituality does not present itself as a closed system, delimited by inflexible dogmas or immutable rules. Instead, it manifests as a fluid and deeply personal path, in which each individual is invited to discover their own way of connecting with the divine, with nature, and with ancestry. It is a journey of self-discovery, where spirituality is intertwined with daily experience, allowing each one to build their own relationship with the mysteries of the universe.

The Celts, peoples who inhabited various regions of Europe from the Iron Age to the Middle Ages, had a visceral connection with the land. For them, nature was not just an environment where life unfolded, but a sacred manifestation of divinity. Every tree, every river, every mountain, and every creature was endowed with a unique energy and a spiritual presence. The cycles of the seasons, birth and death, the renewal of life – all were part of a large interconnected web, where nothing existed in isolation. This awareness of the interconnection between all things permeated their culture, their rituals, and their way of seeing the world.

In the Celtic vision, the universe was not only matter and physical, but also spiritual and invisible. There were subtle forces acting in all aspects of existence, connecting living beings through invisible threads of energy. To honor this interconnection, the Celts held seasonal festivals, told sacred stories, and chanted songs that transmitted ancestral wisdom. In this way, they celebrated the sacredness of life and reinforced the link between the living, the ancestors, and the spirits of nature.

Within this vision, the human soul was considered eternal and cyclical. Each being carried within themselves a divine spark, a sacred essence that transcends time and space. The Celtic soul was understood as a traveler, who traversed various existences, accumulating knowledge and evolving with each experience. Death, therefore, did not represent a definitive end, but a transition – a return to the womb of the Great Mother, where the soul rested and prepared for a new incarnation. The belief in the continuity of life, in constant transformation, and in the renewal of energy was one of the fundamental pillars of this spirituality.

For the Celts, nature was the great teacher. They carefully observed the cycles of the seasons, the movement of the stars, and the behavior of animals, seeking to learn from the rhythms and patterns of the natural world. They believed that every element of nature contained a hidden teaching, waiting to be understood by those who were willing to listen. Trees, in particular, were revered as guardians of knowledge and magical power. Each species possessed a unique energy and was associated with certain spiritual qualities. The druids, Celtic priests and sages, used trees for rituals of healing, divination, and connection with the divinities.

Natural spaces were also considered sacred, as they were seen as points of great concentration of energy. Rivers, lakes, mountains, caves, and forests were places of power, where the veil between the worlds was thinner. In these special places, the Celts held ceremonies, made offerings, and sought spiritual guidance. The relationship with these places was not one of domination or exploitation, but of respect and reverence.

Within Celtic mythology, the gods and goddesses were not distant or inaccessible figures, but living forces that represented different aspects of nature, the human psyche, and the cosmos. Each divinity carried within it characteristics that reflected experiences and challenges of the human journey. By connecting with these gods, we awaken these qualities within ourselves, finding strength, inspiration, and wisdom to face our own internal and external battles.

The goddess Brigid, for example, is one of the most well-known of the Celtic pantheon. Representing fire, poetry, healing, and the art of metalworking, she symbolizes creativity, inspiration, and the ability to transform matter and mind. Her cult is associated with the eternal flame of knowledge and the protection of homes and families. The god Lugh, master of all arts and skilled warrior, is a divinity who embodies excellence, leadership, and the light that dispels darkness. His myth teaches the importance of versatility and the pursuit of continuous improvement.

Celtic rituals were ways of establishing contact with these energies and celebrating the sacredness of existence. Each ceremony was a moment of communion with the divine, with the ancestors, and with the elements of nature. Rituals could vary in complexity, from small individual prayers to large community festivals. However, all shared the goal of creating a sacred space, a time out of time, where it was possible to connect with spiritual forces and receive their guidance.

These rituals not only honored the cycles of nature and the passages of life, but also served as tools of healing and transformation. Through them, the Celts expressed gratitude for the blessings received, sought protection and purification, and strengthened their connection with the mysteries of the universe. The act of participating in a ritual was seen as a commitment to one's own spirituality and a step towards harmonizing with the natural flow of existence.

Those who wished to deepen themselves on this spiritual path needed to understand that this journey was a gradual process. Becoming a disciple of the Celtic tradition required dedication, discipline, and a sincere willingness to learn and evolve. Knowledge was not simply transmitted passively, but rather gained through experience, observation, and constant practice.

In this book, teachings will be presented that will guide the reader through the foundations of Celtic spirituality. You will learn to create sacred spaces, to work with the elements of nature, to honor the gods, and to celebrate the cycles of the year. Each chapter will open a new door to the understanding of this path and will offer practices and reflections that will allow a deeper contact with this ancestral wisdom.

By following this journey, you will become more aware of the interconnection between all things, the presence of the sacred in every aspect of life, and your own divine spark. Celtic spirituality is an invitation to awaken your true potential, to live with more authenticity, and to reconnect with the essence of existence. May the ancient gods guide your steps and may the magic of life always be around you!

Chapter 2
Celtic Cosmovision

The Celtic worldview is an intricate and beautiful system of beliefs that shapes the way ancient Celts viewed the world, time, life, and death. It is a world vision deeply rooted in nature, in the interconnection of all things, and in the belief in multiple realms of existence. Understanding the Celtic worldview is fundamental for any practitioner of Celtic spirituality, as it serves as the basis for all rituals, beliefs, and practices.

The Wheel of the Year was more than a simple calendar for the Celts; it was a reflection of the cycles of nature and of existence itself. For them, time did not advance in a linear way, like a straight path that leads from the past to the future, but rather in circles, always returning to the point of origin, renewing itself in an eternal flow of birth, growth, decline, death, and rebirth. The careful observation of natural patterns – the changing of the seasons, the movement of the stars, the cycles of planting and harvesting – led them to structure the Wheel of the Year in eight main festivals, each representing a specific moment of this cycle and loaded with symbolism and spiritual meaning.

The cycle began with Samhain, celebrated on October 31st, considered the Celtic New Year. It was a period of transition, where the veil between the world of the living and the dead became thinner, allowing communication with ancestors. Communities gathered to honor those who had passed, lighting candles and holding feasts in their memory. It was a time of introspection, marked by the end of the harvest and the preparation for the colder and darker months of the year.

Next came Yule, celebrated on the winter solstice, around December 21st. It was the longest night of the year, but also a moment of hope, as it marked the rebirth of the sun. To celebrate this renewal of light, bonfires and torches were lit, symbolizing the victory of light over darkness. Trees were decorated with symbols of prosperity and protection, a practice that remains alive today in Christmas traditions.

With the arrival of February, Imbolc took place, on the 1st or 2nd of the month. This festival was linked to purification, renewal, and the awakening of life dormant under the ice of winter. It was dedicated to the goddess Brigid, patroness of poetry, healing, and fertility. Candles were lit to illuminate the path of spring, and cleansing rituals were performed, both in the environment and in the spirit.

At the spring equinox, around March 21st, Ostara was celebrated, a period of balance between light and darkness. Nature flourished, and this rebirth was celebrated with the sowing of new intentions, reflecting the growth and fertility of this period. The symbol of the egg, which represents life in potential, was revered, as were hares, animals associated with the goddess Eostre.

The height of spring was marked by Beltane, on May 1st, a vibrant and energy-filled festival that celebrated fertility, passion, and the union of opposites. Sacred fires were lit to purify and strengthen the earth, and young people danced around the Maypole, intertwining colorful ribbons that symbolized the interconnection of life.

At the summer solstice, approximately on June 21st, Litha took place, the festival that celebrated the peak of the sun's power. It was a time of abundance and gratitude for the bounty of nature. Bonfires were lit to strengthen the light and ward off negative influences, and medicinal herbs harvested on this night were considered especially powerful.

The beginning of the harvest was celebrated with Lughnasadh, on August 1st, a time to give thanks for the fruits of the earth and honor the effort of hard work. Named after the god Lugh, this festival included sporting competitions, temporary marriages, and the sharing of the first bread made with the newly harvested grains.

Finally, the autumn equinox, Mabon, around September 21st, marked the balance between day and night. It was a period of introspection and preparation for the approaching winter. The last harvests were carried out, and thanks were given for the food and blessings received throughout the year. As a mirror of Ostara, Mabon symbolized the need for recollection and reflection before the closing of the cycle in Samhain.

These festivals were not just celebrations; they were sacred moments in which the Celts aligned themselves with the rhythms of nature, strengthening their connection with the gods, the spirits, and the very essence of life. Each celebration involved specific rituals, offerings, dances, music, and banquets, creating a deep sense of belonging and continuity.

In addition to the Wheel of the Year, the Celtic worldview recognized the four primordial elements – earth, air, fire, and water – as vital forces that permeated the world and influenced existence. Earth represented stability, nourishment, and security; air symbolized intellect, movement, and communication; fire was associated with transformation, passion, and creativity; and water, with intuition, healing, and emotions. The balance between these elements was essential to maintain harmony in life and in rituals.

Another fundamental concept was the existence of the three interconnected realms: Earth -Talamh-, Sea -Muir-, and Sky -Neamh-. Earth represented the material world, where humans and animals lived and interacted. The Sea was the realm of deep mysteries, emotions, and fluid magic. The Sky, in turn, was the dwelling of the gods and inspiration, a place of wisdom and transcendence. These realms were not separate, but interconnected, and the Celts believed that it was possible to travel between them through dreams, meditation, and rituals.

At the heart of this vision was the web of life, a concept that reflected the interconnection of all things. For the Celts, every thought, action, and word had an impact on the whole, and respecting this balance was fundamental to living in harmony with nature and with other beings.

Beyond the visible world, the Celts also believed in the Other World -Anwynn, Sidhe-, an invisible realm inhabited by gods, ancestors, and fairy beings. This magical plane overlapped with the physical world, especially in sacred places such as forests, hills, and rivers. It was possible to access it through natural portals or altered states of consciousness, and many rituals were performed to honor and communicate with these spiritual forces.

The belief in the journey of the soul was also central to the Celts, who saw death not as an end, but as a transition. Reincarnation was part of this cycle, where the soul returned repeatedly to continue learning and evolving. Death was a return to the womb of the Great Mother, a period of rest before being reborn for a new experience. For this reason, ancestors were deeply revered, as their wisdom remained alive, guiding and protecting the living.

The Celtic worldview, with its richness of symbols and its deep connection with nature, was not just a set of beliefs, but a way of life. It was an invitation to see life as a continuous cycle, where everything is interconnected and where each moment has its own value within the great dance of the universe.

Understanding the Celtic worldview is essential to delve deeper into the spirituality and rituals of this ancient people. It is a world vision rich in symbolism, magic, and wisdom, which invites us to live in harmony with nature, with the cycles of life, and with the sacred web that unites all things. In the next chapters, we will explore how this worldview manifests itself in Celtic rituals and practices.

Chapter 3
Gods and Goddesses

The Celtic pantheon is vast and diverse, reflecting the rich tapestry of cultures and traditions that made up the ancient Celtic world. Far from being a unified system, Celtic divinities vary from region to region, with different names, attributes, and stories. However, certain themes and archetypes emerge, revealing the deep connection of the Celts with nature, fertility, war, sovereignty, and the Otherworld.

The multifaceted nature of Celtic divinities reveals a fundamental aspect of the spirituality of this people: the belief that gods and goddesses were not immutable and fixed figures, but living, fluid, and dynamic forces, which manifested themselves in different ways depending on the context. Unlike many traditions that attribute rigid and anthropomorphic characteristics to the gods, the Celts saw their divinities as expressions of nature itself, incorporating its cycles, its mutations, and its multiple facets. Thus, the same god or goddess could present themselves in distinct ways to different peoples, regions, or moments of life.

This fluidity manifests itself, for example, in the figure of the goddess of sovereignty. Her role was to guarantee the legitimacy of the kings and the prosperity of the lands they ruled. However, her appearance and name changed according to the people who worshiped her. In Ireland, she manifested as Medb, a warrior queen associated with strength, desire, and authority. At another time, she became Ériu, the very personification of the island of Ireland, whose name echoes to this day. In Wales, she took the form of Rhiannon, a goddess linked to fertility, royalty, and the Otherworld. The most interesting thing is that this same goddess could appear sometimes as a seductive and enchanting young woman, sometimes as a powerful mature queen, sometimes as a wise and mysterious old woman, and even in the form of a sacred animal, like a magical mare. These different aspects reveal the Celtic understanding of divine nature as something in constant transformation, reflecting the very cycles of life, death, and rebirth.

Another recurring archetype in Celtic mythology is that of the Mother Goddess, the primordial source of all creation. She represents fertility, nurturing, and the earth that sustains all creatures. In some traditions, she appears under the name of Danu, in Ireland, considered the ancestor of the Tuatha Dé Danann, the mythical people of gods and heroes. In Wales, she is called Dôn, while in Ireland she can also be recognized as Anu. Many times, this goddess assumes a triple form, symbolizing the different phases of life: the maiden, who represents the beginning of the journey and the potential of the new; the mother, who symbolizes creation, abundance, and the power to generate life; and the old woman, guardian of wisdom and deep knowledge.

Alongside her, we find the Horned God, a male divinity associated with vital force, wild nature, and fertility. His most well-known name is Cernunnos, worshiped mainly in Gaul, but he also appears in different versions in England, as Herne, and in Celtic mythology in general, as the Stag King. Represented with deer antlers, he symbolizes the connection with animals, the earth, and the eternal cycle of life and death. His role is not only that of hunter, but also of protector and lord of the natural realms, often being associated with renewal and abundance.

The Celtic pantheon also includes figures like the God of Sovereignty, who protects the tribe and the land, guaranteeing justice and balance. Among the most notable examples are Dagda, the powerful father of the Irish gods, owner of a magic cauldron that never empties, and Nuada, the king who had a silver hand, symbol of his power and legitimacy. Taranis, venerated in Gaul, was a god associated with the sky and thunder, reinforcing his connection with royalty and war.

The God of Light and the Arts emerges as a fascinating archetype, representing creativity, knowledge, and skill in various areas. Lugh, in Ireland, is one of the most venerated, known as a master of all arts, from poetry to war. In Wales, this role is played by Lleu, while in Gaul, he is recognized as Belenos, often linked to the sun and healing.

Brigid, in turn, is one of the most revered names among Celtic divinities. Associated with healing, poetry, and inspiration, she is invoked both as a protector and as a spiritual guide. Over time, her importance was so great that, even after Christianization, she was syncretized in the figure of Saint Brigid, maintaining her role as patroness of the arts and healing.

In addition to these examples, the Celts worshiped gods and goddesses of war, death, and the Otherworld, such as Morrigan, who could appear as a single goddess or as a triad of warrior sisters. These divinities not only symbolized the challenges and transformations of life, but also served as guardians of the mysteries of existence.

For those who wish to connect with these ancestral energies, there is no single path or rigid formula. Contact with Celtic divinities is a personal experience, which can be cultivated in various ways. Study and research are the first essential steps. Knowing the stories, symbols, and myths of the gods and goddesses allows us to understand their manifestations and recognize their presence in everyday life.

Meditation and visualization are powerful practices to establish this connection. By closing your eyes and imagining yourself in a sacred place, such as an ancient forest or a circle of stones, it is possible to visualize the desired divinity and feel its energy. Creating an altar dedicated to these gods is a concrete way to honor them, gathering symbols, offerings, and elements that represent their essence. Candles, incense, images, and sacred foods, such as grains, fruits, and honey, can be used for this purpose.

Rituals also play an important role. From simple prayers and moments of gratitude to more elaborate ceremonies, each gesture of devotion strengthens the bond with the divine. Observing nature is another powerful way to connect with the Celtic gods, since they are living manifestations of natural cycles. Perceiving the seasons, the elements, and the animals around you can reveal subtle messages and signs of the presence of these divinities.

Dreams and intuition are means by which the gods can communicate, sending visions, symbols, or feelings that bring guidance and teachings. Keeping a diary to record these insights can help identify patterns and recognize divine messages. For those who feel called, the practice of shamanic journeys can be a profound way to visit the Otherworld and establish contact with these spiritual entities.

It is essential to remember that each person has a unique affinity with certain divinities, and this connection must be respected and cultivated with authenticity. Honoring one's own ancestors also strengthens this bond, as they often act as intermediaries between the human and the divine world. Above all, the important thing is that this journey be lived with sincerity, without clinging to dogmas or fixed formulas. The Celtic gods are free, dynamic, and transforming forces, and our relationship with them must reflect this same freedom.

Celtic spirituality is not based on absolute truths, but on personal experiences, natural cycles, and the deep connection between man and the sacred. Whoever walks this path finds not only knowledge and inspiration, but also a reunion with himself and with the mystery of the universe.

The connection with Celtic divinities is a journey of discovery, learning, and growth. It is a path that leads us to a deeper understanding of ourselves, of nature, and of the divine. May this chapter be a guide in your journey of connection with the Celtic gods and goddesses. May you find inspiration, wisdom, and blessings on your way.

Chapter 4
Sacred Spaces

In Celtic spirituality, nature is not merely a backdrop, but a living temple, pulsing with divine energy. The Celts recognized the inherent sacredness of the natural world and created sacred spaces to honor this energy, connect with the deities, and perform rituals. These spaces could be natural or constructed, permanent or temporary, but all shared the characteristic of being portals between worlds, places where the veil between the visible and invisible became thinner.

The sacredness of nature was a fundamental principle for the Celts, who saw the natural world as a direct manifestation of the divine. They did not need grandiose temples built by human hands, as they considered the earth itself a living temple. Majestic trees, dense forests, serene rivers, crystalline springs, imposing mountains, mysterious caves, ancient rocks, as well as the celestial bodies – the sun, the moon, and the stars – all were imbued with a deep spiritual significance. For the Celts, every element of nature possessed a sacred essence and was intrinsically linked to the cycles of life and the universe.

This view contrasts sharply with the modern mentality, which often sees nature as a resource to be exploited or a challenge to be overcome. However, for the ancient Celts, the earth was a teacher, a guide, and an inexhaustible source of healing and inspiration. They saw themselves as an integral part of nature, never separate from it, and sought to harmonize with its rhythms and cycles. The changing of the seasons, the flow of the waters, the blowing of the winds, and the brilliance of the stars were not merely natural phenomena, but manifestations of spiritual forces that governed the world.

Thus, the Celts identified and respected spaces where the energy of the earth manifested more intensely. These sacred places could be forests, springs, mountains, caves, or unusually shaped stones, considered portals to other planes of existence. Each of these spaces was used for specific purposes, whether for healing rituals, offerings to the divinities, meditations, or celebrations of the cycles of life.

The sacred forests, called Nemeton, were regarded as true natural temples. Millennial trees, especially oaks, ashes, and yews, were venerated as dwellings of spirits and gods. The druids, Celtic priests and wise men, held ceremonies and transmitted their knowledge in these sacred forests, where the connection between the physical and spiritual worlds was stronger.

Sacred springs and wells were places of deep reverence, as it was believed that their waters possessed healing and purifying properties. These waters were seen as a manifestation of the feminine energies of the earth, linked to the goddesses of fertility and healing. As a form of devotion, people left coins, flowers, and personal objects in these places, seeking blessings and protection.

Mountains and hills also occupied a central role in Celtic spirituality. They were considered abodes of the gods, places of great power and spiritual vision. Climbing to the top of a sacred mountain was an act of pilgrimage, a journey in search of wisdom and connection with the divine. Many hills and mountains were associated with ancient legends and myths, being considered portals to the Otherworld.

Caves and grottoes possessed a deep symbolism in Celtic culture. They were seen as passages to hidden realms, places of mystery, transformation, and rebirth. Many of them were used for initiation rituals and meditation practices, providing a space for introspection and contact with the ancestors.

The sacred stones were also highly respected. Unusual rock formations, monoliths, and dolmens were considered landmarks of ancestral power, places where the energy of the earth was concentrated. Many of these stones were adorned with Celtic symbols, such as spirals, triskeles, and knots, engraved to amplify their connection with the spiritual world.

Although nature was their primary temple, the Celts also built sacred structures for specific purposes. The stone circles, such as the famous megalithic monuments of Stonehenge and Avebury, are impressive examples of this tradition. It is believed that these circles were used for religious ceremonies, celebrations of the solar and lunar cycles, rites of passage, and astronomical observations.

The mounds —sídhe—, in turn, were earth structures built over tombs or places considered sacred. Associated with the Otherworld, they were seen as portals to fairy realms and abodes of the ancestors. Many Celtic myths speak of magical beings that inhabited these mounds, giving them an enigmatic and supernatural character.

Altars were commonly erected both in natural spaces and in homes and meeting places. Made of stone or wood, they served as points of offerings, where food, flowers, herbs, and other items were deposited to honor the gods and spirits. In these structures, prayers were made and rituals were conducted with deep respect and devotion.

Inspired by this ancestral wisdom, it is possible to create a sacred space in our own homes or gardens, where we can reconnect with our divine essence and with nature. For this, some steps can be followed:

First, choose a place that transmits peace and inspiration. It can be a corner of the room, a sunny balcony, a flowery garden, or even a nook in the midst of nature. The next step is to clean and purify the environment, both physically and energetically. Removing unnecessary objects, sweeping the floor, and cleaning surfaces help to create a harmonious space. Then, you can use incense, salt water, sounds of bells, or visualizations of light to eliminate stagnant energies and strengthen the vibration of the place.

To delimit this sacred space, you can use stones, shells, candles, crystals, or fabrics. This demarcation helps to create an energetic boundary between the spiritual and the everyday. In the center, you can erect an altar with symbolic elements of Celtic spirituality, such as images of deities, candles, crystals, herbs, offerings, and natural objects.

After organizing the altar, the space can be consecrated through a prayer or declaration of intent. You can recite a mantra, sing a song, or simply express in words the desire to use that space for connection with the sacred. The frequent use of this environment strengthens its energy, making it increasingly conducive to meditation, rituals, and spiritual reflections.

In addition to fixed spaces, the Celts also used a powerful concept: the sacred circle, a way to create a portable sacred space. The circle, symbol of totality and protection, was drawn on the ground to delimit a safe and spiritualized environment. Its creation process involved some fundamental steps.

First, a quiet place was chosen where one could remain without interruptions. Then, the purification of the space and of the person participating in the ritual was carried out, using incense or salt water. The circle was then delimited physically, with stones, branches, or ropes, or visualized energetically as a barrier of light. When walking around the circle clockwise –deosil–, this energy was imagined to be expanding and creating a protection around it.

After this preparation, the natural elements and the divinities were invited to participate. Earth, air, fire, and water were called to offer their energy and protection. The Celtic divinities, according to the spiritual connection of each one, were invoked to guide and strengthen the ritual.

During the ceremony, the sacred circle kept the energy high and protected those who were inside it. At the end of the ritual, the elements and deities were thanked for their presence and, slowly, the circle was undone. It was walked around it in the counterclockwise direction –tuathail–, visualizing its energy dissipating and returning to the natural flow of the universe.

This ancestral practice remains a powerful instrument of spiritual connection, allowing anyone, anywhere, to create a sacred space and strengthen their connection with nature and the divine.

The sacred circle is a powerful tool for Celtic spiritual practice, allowing you to create a sacred space anywhere and at any time.

Chapter 5
Ritualistic Preparation

The preparation for a Celtic ritual is as important as the ritual itself. It is a time to disconnect from the profane world, to purify oneself, to protect oneself, and to connect with the subtle energies that will be invoked. Careful preparation increases the effectiveness of the ritual and ensures a deeper and more meaningful experience.

Before any Celtic ritual, the purification of the body and energy is essential to ensure that the connection with the sacred is full and unencumbered. The first step in this process is physical cleansing, which can be done in several ways. The ritual bath, for example, is one of the most effective methods for this purification. It should be taken with intention, allowing the water to carry away all impurities, both physical and spiritual. To enhance this effect, you can add ingredients to the bath such as coarse salt, which is a powerful energy purifier, as well as herbs such as rosemary, sage, and lavender, which bring protection, clarity, and tranquility. If you prefer, a few drops of essential oils of these same herbs can be added to the water, intensifying the sensory and vibrational experience of the bath. During this time, it is important to visualize the impurities being washed away and dissolved by the water, allowing only renewed energy to remain.

Another beneficial practice for physical cleansing is dry brushing. Using a natural bristle brush, gently rub the dry skin in circular motions, always directing the movements towards the heart. This technique not only removes dead cells, revitalizing the skin, but also stimulates blood circulation and promotes the release of stagnant energy. It is a simple but very effective method to prepare the body for a ritual.

In addition to bathing and brushing, the choice of clothing is another relevant aspect. Ideally, wear clean clothes, preferably made of natural fabrics such as cotton, linen, or wool. These materials allow energy to flow freely and are more compatible with spiritual practices. In addition, the colors of clothing can be chosen according to the intention of the ritual: white for purification, green for healing, red for passion, blue for intuition, among other possibilities. To reinforce this preparation, it is recommended that these clothes be reserved exclusively for rituals, thus absorbing the energy of the practices over time.

Energy cleansing is also fundamental to remove negative influences and create a vibrational field conducive to the ritual. Smudging is one of the most traditional and powerful techniques for this purpose. Using sacred herbs such as white sage, rosemary, cedar, or palo santo, light the chosen herb and allow the smoke to envelop the body, the altar, and the ritual space. During this process, it is essential to visualize all negative energies being dissipated by the smoke, leaving behind only a clean and sacred atmosphere.

Another form of energy purification is the use of sound. Bells, drums, Tibetan bowls, or even the sound of one's own clapping can be used to break up and disperse dense and stagnant energies. The sound resonates in frequencies that reorganize the energy field, preparing it to receive the intentions of the ritual.

Visualization is also a powerful tool in this process. By imagining a white or golden light enveloping the body, the altar, and the ritual space, a shield of protection and purification is created, strengthening the connection with the sacred. To complement this, you can sprinkle water with salt around the space and on yourself, a simple but extremely effective practice to dissipate any unwanted energy.

With the body and the environment properly purified, it is necessary to establish energy protection to avoid unwanted external influences. One of the most effective ways to do this is through visualization. By imagining a sphere of light around yourself, you create a protective barrier that prevents negative energies from approaching. This sphere can be reinforced by invoking spiritual guides, gods, goddesses, ancestors, or guardian angels, asking them to be present and offer protection throughout the ritual.

In addition, symbols of protection can be used to strengthen this energy shield. The triskele, the triquetra, the Celtic cross, and the pentagram are examples of symbols that can be drawn on the body, on candles, on stones, or on pieces of paper to amplify protection. Crystals also play a fundamental role in this process. Stones such as black tourmaline, obsidian, black cyanite, and tiger's eye are known for their protective properties and can be carried with you, placed on the altar, or distributed throughout the ritual space.

For those who practice rituals within a magic circle, the very creation of the circle serves as a powerful barrier against external influences. It delimits a sacred space, warding off any unwanted energy and ensuring a safe environment for spiritual practice.

The choice of clothing is also part of the ritualistic preparation and should be done carefully. In addition to natural fabrics and colors that represent different intentions, the simplicity of the clothing is an important factor. Ritual clothing should be comfortable and allow free movement, avoiding distractions and discomfort during the ritual. Adornments such as necklaces, bracelets, rings, or tiaras can be used, as long as they have a special meaning and are aligned with the intention of the ritual. These objects can be consecrated beforehand so that they carry a specific energy, thus becoming extensions of the practitioner's own energy.

The ritualistic tools, in turn, are essential aids in channeling energies and executing the ritual. The athame, a ritualistic dagger with two edges, is widely used to direct energy, draw the magic circle, and cut energy ties, but never to cut physical objects. The wand, traditionally made of willow, hazel, or oak wood, is another fundamental instrument, being used to invoke the elements and establish connections with nature.

The chalice, representing the water element and the feminine principle, can contain different sacred liquids, such as water, wine, or natural juices, depending on the purpose of the ritual. The pentacle, a plate usually made of wood, metal, or clay, bears the symbol of the pentagram and represents the earth element, the connection with the material world, and the union of the four elements. The cauldron, symbol of the Mother Goddess, is used in various practices, from burning herbs to preparing potions or ritual foods.

Other elements such as incense, candles, and crystals contribute to raising the vibration of the space, while musical instruments such as drums and rattles can be used to induce altered states of consciousness and facilitate connection with the spiritual. However, it is important to remember that none of these tools have power in themselves; their strength lies in the intention and energy that the practitioner places in them.

Finally, before starting the ritual, it is essential to establish a clear connection with the intention of the work to be done. Reflecting on the purpose of the ritual, defining which energies will be invoked, and establishing a precise focus makes the practice much more effective. A good strategy is to write the intention on a piece of paper, meditate on it, or verbalize it aloud. This mental and emotional clarity enhances the results, ensuring that the energy is directed correctly.

Following all these steps is not just a formality, but an act of respect for the gods, the ancestors, and oneself. The ritualistic preparation creates a deep attunement with the sacred, allowing the experience to be truly transformative.

Ritualistic preparation is a process of tuning, of aligning with the subtle energies, and of creating a sacred space inside and out. By carefully preparing for a ritual, you show respect for the gods, the ancestors, and yourself, and open the way for a magical and transformative experience.

Chapter 6
Celtic Symbols

Celtic symbols are more than mere decorations; they are keys to a complex system of beliefs, philosophy, and magic. Each symbol carries a wealth of meanings, often interconnected, that reflect the deep connection of the Celts with nature, the cycles of life, and the spiritual world. By understanding these symbols, we open doors to ancestral wisdom and the practice of Celtic spirituality.

The language of Celtic symbols transcends mere aesthetics; they are portals of power, knowledge, and spirituality. Unlike civilizations that recorded their history in texts, the Celts relied on oral tradition and the visual strength of their symbols to preserve and transmit their wisdom. These signs were engraved on stones, wood, metals, and even tattooed on the skin, carrying profound meanings that went beyond the visible.

More than mere graphic representations, Celtic symbols were magical tools, used in rituals, spells, divination, and protection. Many believed that these geometric shapes and interlacings had the ability to channel cosmic energies and open doors to the Otherworld, connecting practitioners to the divine forces of nature and the universal flow of existence.

Among the most well-known symbols is the Triskle -or Triskelion-, a design composed of three interconnected spirals, representing the cyclical and infinite movement of life. Each curve symbolizes an essential triad within the Celtic worldview: birth, death, and rebirth; earth, sea, and sky; body, mind, and spirit. In addition, the triskle is associated with the Triple Goddess -Maiden, Mother, and Crone- who rules the cycles of life and female wisdom. This symbol was often used to attract dynamic energy, stimulate personal transformation, and represent spiritual evolution.

Another sign of great strength is the Triquetra, a knot of three intertwined arcs, without beginning or end. This symbol also carries the concept of trinity, being linked both to the Triple Goddess and to the natural elements - earth, air, and water, united by fire. In addition to representing eternity and the interconnectedness of all things, the triquetra was considered a powerful amulet of protection, promoting balance and spiritual unity.

The Celtic Cross, in turn, unites pagan and Christian symbolism. With a circle surrounding the cross, it represents the fusion of the divine and the earthly, the axis that links heaven and earth. Its four extremities point to the cardinal directions and the natural elements - fire, earth, air, and water - while the circle reinforces the idea of the continuous cycle of life and time. After the Christianization of the Celtic lands, this cross became an emblem of the Christian faith, but without losing its ancestral roots.

Celtic Knots are patterns of infinite interlacings, symbolizing eternity and the interconnectedness of all things. Without beginning or end, these knots represent the continuity of life, the connection between beings, and spiritual strength. They were used as amulets of protection, symbols of eternal love, and even as marks of commitment in wedding alliances.

The Tree of Life -Crann Bethadh- occupies a central place in Celtic mythology. Its deep roots in the underworld, its trunk on earth, and its branches extending to the sky make it a bridge between the three worlds. For the Celts, the tree was a symbol of strength, growth, wisdom, and ancestry. In rituals, it was revered as a source of power and spiritual connection.

Another striking symbol is the Spiral, which frequently appears in Celtic art. It represents growth, the expansion of consciousness, and the cycles of life. Its continuous movement symbolizes the inner journey in search of self-knowledge and spiritual enlightenment. It is often associated with cosmic energy and the vital flow of the universe.

Finally, the Awen, composed of three rays of light emanating from a central point, represents divine inspiration. Its origin lies in the Druidic tradition, where it symbolized the connection with universal wisdom and the balance between opposing forces - light and darkness, masculine and feminine, rational mind and intuition. For those who follow the Celtic spiritual path, the Awen is a call to the search for knowledge and harmony.

These symbols can be integrated into spiritual practice in various ways. Meditation with a Celtic symbol, for example, helps to absorb its energy and understand its teachings. The placement of amulets or talismans with these signs on the altar or in personal jewelry reinforces the connection with their protective forces. Arts and crafts inspired by these sacred forms also serve as a way to honor this tradition.

In rituals, drawing a symbol on the ground, on candles, or on the body itself can enhance its magical intention. Those who feel a deeper calling may even choose to tattoo a Celtic symbol, always taking into account its meaning before marking the skin with an emblem of ancestral power.

Regardless of how they are used, Celtic symbols continue to be portals to ancient wisdom, connecting practitioners with the energy of the universe and with the spirituality of their ancestors. By working with them with respect and awareness, it is possible to access their strength and transform one's spiritual journey.

When working with Celtic symbols, remember that they are more than simple designs. They are portals to ancestral wisdom, keys to magic and connection with the divine. Use them with respect, intention, and awareness.

Chapter 7
Ogham
The Oracle

Ogham -pronounced "oh-am" or "og-am"- is an ancient Celtic writing system, often called the "alphabet of trees." More than just an alphabet, Ogham is an oracle, a divinatory system and a magical tool, deeply connected to nature and the wisdom of the druids.

The origin of Ogham dates back to ancient times and involves a mixture of history and mystery. Although its exact creation remains uncertain, many scholars believe it originated in Ireland around the 4th century AD. The oldest inscriptions have been found on stones and monuments, scattered mainly throughout Ireland and Wales, suggesting that its use was both practical and ceremonial. These inscriptions usually recorded names of people, clans, and places, being used to mark borders or pay homage to deceased individuals. However, the true importance of Ogham transcends its written function, as it was considered sacred knowledge, transmitted orally by the druids, the Celtic sages and priests. For them, Ogham was not only an alphabet, but also a system of divination, a magical tool and a channel of communication with the spiritual world.

The structure of Ogham is unique and distinct. It is composed of 20 main letters, known as feda -in the singular, fid-, each of which is associated with a sacred tree or plant. The writing form of Ogham is based on straight or diagonal strokes carved along a central line called druim, which can be the edge of a stone or the surface of a piece of wood. The feda are organized into four groups of five letters, called aicme -singular, aicme-, and each of these groups is named after the first corresponding letter. The first group, Aicme Beithe, includes the letters B, L, F, S, and N, associated with birch, ash, alder, willow, and hawthorn, respectively. Aicme hÚatha comprises the letters H, D, T, C, and Q, linked to hawthorn, oak, fir, poplar, and yew. Aicme Muine is composed of the letters M, G, NG, Z, and R, representing vine, ivy, reed, blackthorn, and dwarf birch or alder. Finally, Aicme Ailme encompasses the letters A, O, U, E, and I, connected to silver fir, gorse, heather, white poplar or aspen, and strawberry tree or yew. In addition to these 20 fundamental letters, there are also five additional letters called forfeda, which were introduced later to expand the system.

Ogham was also widely used as an oracle, a divinatory method employed by the druids to access the wisdom of trees and nature spirits. Like the Norse runes or the Chinese I Ching, the practice of divination with Ogham had different methods. One of the most traditional was the throwing of rods: small wooden rods, each with a fid engraved, were thrown onto a flat surface, and the way they fell was interpreted according to the visible letters. Another common method involved choosing rods from within a bag or container. The consultant formulated a question, withdrew one or more rods and interpreted the drawn feda. There was also the practice of drawing cards, where cards containing the Ogham symbols were used in a similar way to the Tarot, being shuffled and drawn to obtain answers. In addition, meditating with a specific fid was another powerful method for receiving insights and intuitive guidance, allowing the practitioner to connect deeply with the energy of the corresponding tree.

In addition to the divinatory function, Ogham was a magical tool used to influence the world around. Its letters were considered symbols of power, capable of channeling energies and manifesting intentions. A common practice was the making of talismans and amulets, in which the feda were engraved for specific purposes, such as protection, healing, and prosperity. The druids also employed the feda in enchantments and spells, combining the symbols with words of power and rituals to realize desires and intentions. Another magical application of Ogham involved connecting with the energy of trees, allowing practitioners to invoke their spirits and work with the forces of nature. In seasonal rituals, the letters of Ogham were aligned with different periods of the Celtic Wheel of the Year, being used to mark moments of transition and celebration.

Each tree associated with Ogham has a specific symbolic meaning and spiritual properties. The birch - Beithe- represents new beginnings, purification, and renewal, being a tree of protection and growth. The ash - Luis- is linked to strength, healing, and connection with the Otherworld. The alder -Fearn- symbolizes courage, protection, and guidance, while the willow -Saille- is associated with intuition, emotions, and flexibility. The hawthorn -Nuin- represents challenges, purification, and overcoming obstacles. The rowan -Huath- is a symbol of love, marriage, and fertility, often related to sacred ceremonies. The oak -Duir- is a tree of strength, wisdom, and stability, considered a portal to the spiritual world. The fir -Tinne- represents balance and resilience, while the poplar -Coll- is linked to knowledge, communication, and inspiration. The yew -Quert- symbolizes death and rebirth, transformation and protection against negative energies. Other important trees include the vine -Muin-, related to celebration and fertility; the ivy -Gort-, which represents growth and overcoming; the reed -nGéadal-, associated with healing and adaptability; and the blackthorn -Straif-, which symbolizes protection and resistance. Each of these trees has a unique energy and can be worked with spiritually to align with natural forces.

Ogham can be incorporated into spiritual practice in various ways. Studying and researching its history, structure, and symbolism are fundamental to understanding its depth. Creating your own set of Ogham, whether in wooden rods or illustrated cards, can be a meaningful way to connect with this tradition. The practice of divination with Ogham is another powerful way to gain spiritual guidance, whether through drawing rods, throwing them on a surface, or reading cards. Meditating with a specific fid allows you to deepen your connection with its energy, visualizing the corresponding tree and absorbing its wisdom. Talismans and amulets can be made with the feda, carrying specific intentions and serving as symbols of protection and balance. During rituals, the letters of Ogham can be drawn on the ground, carved into candles, or traced on the body as a form of consecration and energy strengthening. Furthermore, spending time in nature, observing and interacting with the trees associated with Ogham, is a practical and spiritual way to honor this ancestral tradition.

Ogham is, therefore, more than a simple writing system: it is a portal to the wisdom of the ancient Celts, a tool for connecting with nature and the divine. By exploring its mysteries, it is possible to enrich spiritual practice and develop a deeper understanding of the natural world and its interaction with the spiritual universe.

Ogham is a portal to the ancestral wisdom of the Celts, a tool for connecting with nature and the divine. By exploring its mysteries, you can enrich your spiritual practice and deepen your understanding of the world around you.

Chapter 8
Natural Magic

Natural magic is one of the pillars of Celtic spirituality, a practice that is based on the belief that nature is a source of power, healing, and wisdom. The Celts lived in close relationship with the natural world, and their magic was an extension of that relationship. They believed that every element of nature – plants, stones, water, air, fire – possessed a vital energy, a spiritual force that could be accessed and used for various purposes.

Celtic natural magic does not seek to dominate or subjugate nature, but rather to establish a bond of respect and harmony with it. For the Celts, everything was part of a large interconnected fabric, where every action reverberated in the balance of the whole. Thus, when practicing natural magic, it was not just an isolated act, but an energetic exchange with the universe, a cycle of respect and reciprocity.

The basis of this magic is founded on essential principles. The first of these is the understanding that everything is energy. The Celts believed that every element, every living being, and even thoughts and emotions possessed their own vibration, capable of being influenced and directed by intention and will.

Likewise, nature was considered sacred, a living manifestation of the divine. Every tree, stone, river and mountain carried a spark of primordial energy and, therefore, should be revered.

Another fundamental concept was interconnection. Just as the branches of a tree grow from a common trunk, all beings were linked, and any change in this balance was reflected in the whole. From this vision arose the belief in the Law of Attraction, which stated that similar energies attract each other. Positive thoughts and well-directed intentions would attract favorable situations, while negative emotions would tend to bring obstacles. In addition, the Triple Law reinforced the idea that everything sent to the world would return multiplied by three, whether a blessing or a curse. This belief encouraged a conscious use of magic, with responsibility for the consequences of one's own actions.

Finally, one of the most important pillars of Celtic magic was respect and reciprocity. Nothing should be taken from nature without something being offered in return. A branch harvested, a stone used in a spell, or even the water from a river, everything needed to be honored with an offering, a gesture of gratitude, so that balance was maintained.

Within this vision of respect and connection with nature, working with the elements played a central role. The four elements – earth, air, fire and water – were not just physical manifestations, but living forces, endowed with unique properties, which could be invoked and directed for different purposes.

Earth represented stability, nourishment and growth. It was the element of prosperity, of the materialization of desires and connection with ancestral roots. Its correspondences included the north, winter, night and the physical body, as well as the mineral kingdom, with its stones and crystals. To work with this element, the Celts cultivated sacred gardens, buried objects to establish intentions, and meditated in nature, absorbing its energy.

Air, in turn, symbolized communication, intellect and inspiration. Associated with the east, spring and dawn, this element was linked to clear thinking, innovative ideas and intuition. Working with air involved practices such as writing spells, singing ritual songs, using feathers in rituals, and burning incense whose smoke carried wishes to the universe.

Fire was the spark of transformation, courage and action. Linked to the south, summer and noon, this element was related to passion and creativity. To activate its energy, the Celts lit bonfires in sacred celebrations, used candles in rituals, and worked with the strength of the sun, absorbing its vitality.

Water, on the other hand, was the element of emotions, intuition and purification. Representing the west, autumn and dusk, it carried the flow of life, promoting healing and renewal. To connect with this element, the Celts performed ritual baths, prepared potions, practiced divination by observing the surface of the water, and offered gifts to rivers and lakes.

In addition to the elements, plants played a fundamental role in Celtic magic. The druids were profound connoisseurs of their medicinal and spiritual properties, using them both for healing and for spells and rituals. Herbology allowed them to understand which plants could be used to restore health, balance energies, and create protective amulets.

Potions, prepared from herbs, roots, flowers and other natural ingredients, were used for various purposes, such as attracting prosperity, strengthening love, or providing mental clarity. Likewise, incense was a powerful tool for purification and energetic elevation, being burned in rituals to create a connection with the gods. Ointments, made from the infusion of herbs in vegetable oils, were applied to the body to intensify meditative states and aid in the spiritual journey.

Crystals, although less used than plants, were also considered powerful allies. Each stone possessed a unique vibration, capable of influencing energetic fields and assisting in the realization of desires. Clear quartz was widely valued for its ability to amplify intentions, while amethyst was used for protection and spiritual development. Citrine attracted prosperity, rose quartz favored love, and black tourmaline functioned as a shield against negative energies.

Water, in addition to being an essential element, possessed its own magic. Springs, rivers and lakes were considered sacred places, meeting points between the physical and spiritual world. Ritual baths were performed for purification and renewal, while divination was practiced by observing the surface of the water, seeking images and hidden messages. As a way to honor the spirits of the waters, offerings were left, often in the form of coins, flowers or small symbolic objects.

Fire, in turn, possessed a special connection with the Celts. Bonfires were lit during festivals like Beltane and Samhain, serving as portals to the Otherworld and symbols of renewal. Candles also played an essential role, being used to illuminate paths and manifest intentions. The sun, seen as a source of vital power, was celebrated in solstices and equinoxes, reinforcing its importance in Celtic magic.

Air, being the element of intellect and communication, had its power accessed through the use of incense, feathers and conscious breathing practices. The smoke of the incense carried prayers and requests, while the feathers were used as symbols of lightness and freedom. Conscious breathing, a technique similar to pranayama, was used to balance emotions and strengthen vital energy.

For those who wish to initiate themselves into Celtic natural magic, some steps can be followed. The first is to study and research, understanding the culture, mythology and practices of this ancestral people. Next, it is essential to develop a connection with nature, observing its cycles and learning to perceive its subtle messages. Intuition should be worked on constantly, as it is an essential tool to direct magical practice. Starting with simple actions, such as lighting candles, meditating in nature and making offerings, is a good way to become familiar with the energy of the elements.

Respect for nature must be constant, never taking anything without permission and always giving back in some way. Creativity is another important point, as natural magic does not follow rigid rules, allowing for adaptations and customizations. Above all, trusting the process and one's own spiritual growth is essential. Celtic magic is a path of continuous learning, where each experience strengthens the bond with the natural world and with the divine.

Practicing Celtic natural magic means walking in harmony with the rhythms of the Earth, honoring its wisdom and absorbing its energy. This path allows you to access the sacred essence of the universe and, through it, bring more balance, healing and enchantment to your own life.

Celtic natural magic is a path of reconnection with nature, with our divine essence and with ancestral wisdom. By practicing it, we can bring more balance, healing, beauty and magic to our lives.

Part II: Rites of the Wheel of the Year

Chapter 9
Samhain
Honoring the Ancestors

Samhain -pronounced "so-in" or "sah-win"- is the Celtic festival that marks the end of summer and the beginning of winter, the end of the harvest and the beginning of the Celtic new year. Celebrated on October 31st, Samhain is a time of transition, when the veil between the world of the living and the world of the dead becomes thinner. It is a time to honor the ancestors, celebrate the harvest, reflect on the past and prepare for the future.

Samhain, whose meaning comes from Gaelic as "end of summer," was for the Celts a moment of extreme importance. With the arrival of winter, the harvests were stored, the cattle were gathered and the preparations for the cold season intensified. But this festival went beyond agricultural issues: it represented a period of deep spirituality, where the veil between the worlds became thinner, allowing the spirits of the ancestors to visit the world of the living. This contact with the Other World aroused ambiguous feelings in the Celts: respect and veneration for the ancestors, but also fear of the unknown, as the spirits could bring messages, but also mischief.

It was a time of celebration and mourning, of joy and introspection. The rituals performed had the purpose of honoring those who came before and preparing for the cycle of death and rebirth that the arrival of winter symbolized. And even today, many of these practices can be incorporated to keep alive the connection with our ancestors and with the natural cycles of life.

For those who wish to celebrate Samhain in an authentic way, there are several rituals that can be performed, adapted to individual circumstances. Among them, one of the most significant is the creation of an altar dedicated to the ancestors. Choosing a special place in the house and covering it with a dark fabric, such as black, purple or brown, already helps to create an environment conducive to spiritual connection. In this space, arranging photos of the ancestors, or, if there are no images available, objects that can represent them, such as jewelry, letters, tools or personal items, reinforces this bond. Candles are lit in honor of the deceased, with white or black being the most traditional, although other colors can be used according to each one's intuition. Offerings of food and drinks, such as bread, fruits, cakes, milk, wine or beer, are placed on the altar, as well as incenses of sage, rosemary, myrrh or frankincense, which help to purify the space and make it receptive to the energies of the ancestors. Spending time in front of the altar, in silence or meditation, remembering stories, thanking the presence of those who came before and asking for their guidance, becomes a moment of deep connection.

Another way to honor the ancestors during Samhain is to prepare a special meal in their honor. The ideal is to cook dishes that were part of the family tradition or that were appreciated by those who have already left. During dinner, an extra place is set at the table, symbolizing the presence of the spirits, and in it are served the same foods and drinks consumed by the living. While sharing stories and memories, the life of those who have left is celebrated, honoring their legacy. The food and drink left in the place of the ancestors remain there for a while after the meal, as an offering, and only then are discarded in a respectful manner, returning them to nature or depositing them in an appropriate place.

If there is the possibility, lighting a bonfire outdoors is another powerful ritual. Fire symbolizes purification, transformation and connection with the Other World. Around the flames, it is possible to meditate, sing, dance or simply observe the fire consuming sacred herbs, such as sage, rosemary or laurel, which can be thrown into the bonfire as offerings. You can also write messages to the ancestors on small pieces of paper and burn them, allowing the words to be carried by the smoke to the spiritual world. In addition, the bonfire is an excellent opportunity to visualize the fire consuming negative energies, fears and worries, opening space for new beginnings.

As Samhain is a propitious moment for divination, due to the weakening of the barrier between the worlds, this is an ideal time to consult oracles and seek guidance. The Tarot, the runes, the Ogham, the reading of coffee grounds or the clairvoyance on reflective surfaces, such as water or a mirror, are some of the methods that can be used. Formulating questions about the future, asking for advice from the ancestors or seeking answers to personal dilemmas are traditional practices on this night of spiritual connection.

Another important ritual of Samhain is that of liberation. As the celebration marks the closing of a cycle and the beginning of another, it is an ideal time to let go of everything that no longer serves. Writing on a paper the fears, resentments, limiting beliefs or habits that you wish to abandon is a first step. Then, burning this paper in the bonfire or in a cauldron, visualizing the words being transformed into ashes and carried away by the wind, represents the symbolic act of liberation. By getting rid of what weighs, you create space for new opportunities and renew energy for the next cycle.

For those who feel comfortable, visiting a cemetery or a memorial site can also be a respectful way to honor the ancestors. Bringing flowers, lighting candles or simply spending time in silence next to the grave of loved ones are gestures of affection and respect. If necessary, cleaning the place and dedicating a few moments to thank and talk with those who have left strengthens the link between the worlds.

Finally, the connection with nature is essential in Samhain. Being a festival of transition between the seasons, spending time outdoors, observing the subtle changes in the landscape, helps to tune in to the natural rhythm of the Earth. Walking through a forest, feeling the cold wind on your face, observing the leaves falling and realizing how everything follows the flow of life and death are ways of integrating with the natural cycle. Thanking nature for its gifts and asking for its guidance for the new cycle that begins reinforces this connection.

Although Samhain has deep roots in Celtic culture, its rituals can be adapted to modern life and to the personal beliefs of each one. It is not necessary to follow the ancient traditions to the letter; the most important thing is the intention behind each gesture. If there is no space for a bonfire, candles can replace it. If it is not possible to create a large altar, a small space on a table or shelf is enough. What really matters is respect for the ancestors and the search for an authentic meaning.

Many of the traditions associated with Halloween have their origin in Samhain, but, over the centuries, they have been secularized and commercialized. The costumes, the carved pumpkins and the "trick-or-treat" are vestiges of this ancient celebration, although they have lost part of their original meaning. For those who wish to celebrate Samhain in a genuine way, the focus should be the reverence to the ancestors, the connection with nature and the reflection on the cycles of life.

By adopting these rituals, even if in an adapted way, Samhain can become a powerful moment of introspection, transformation and renewal. Celebrating those who came before, thanking for the past and opening oneself to the future with courage and wisdom are ways of honoring this millenary tradition and keeping its legacy alive.

Samhain is a powerful moment of connection, reflection and transformation. By honoring your ancestors and connecting with the energy of this sacred night, you can prepare yourself for the new cycle that begins, release the past and embrace the future with wisdom and courage.

Chapter 10
Yule
The Winter Solstice

Yule, also known as the Winter Solstice, is the celebration of the shortest day and the longest night of the year, marking the turning point when sunlight begins to gradually return. In the northern hemisphere, it occurs around December 21st; in the southern hemisphere, around June 21st. For the Celts and other pagan cultures, Yule was a time of great importance, symbolizing the rebirth of the sun, hope, renewal, and the promise of light and warmth after the darkness of winter.

The origin of the name "Yule" dates back to Germanic and Norse traditions, and although its exact meaning remains uncertain, scholars associate it with the Old Norse word "jól," which means "wheel." This connection refers to the wheel of the year and the eternal cycle of seasons, in which the darkness of winter gives way to the light of the rising sun. Another interpretation suggests that "Yule" derives from "iul," which means "feast" or "celebration," which reinforces the importance of this period as a time of joy and sharing.

Regardless of its etymology, Yule has always been a time of festivity, an interval of light in the middle of the longest night of the year. For the Celts and other pagan peoples, this celebration symbolized the rebirth of the Sun God from the womb of the Earth Mother Goddess. This mythological vision gave a profound meaning to the date: it was the moment when the promise of renewal came to fruition, bringing hope, fertility, and warmth for the months to come.

During Yule, communities gathered to strengthen bonds, share food, and light bonfires and candles, ensuring that the flame of life continued to burn until the return of spring. Homes were adorned with branches of evergreen plants, such as pine, holly, ivy, and mistletoe, symbols of the vitality that persisted even in the most adverse conditions. This time was, above all, a reminder that, even in the depths of winter, the promise of light never faded.

The rituals of Yule had the purpose of greeting the rebirth of the sun, celebrating the continuity of life, and preparing for the new cycle that was beginning. Many of these traditions can be incorporated into the present day, creating a spiritual connection with ancient customs.

To begin with, decorating the house with green plants is a simple but powerful way to bring the energy of rebirth to the environment. The Celts believed that these plants contained a vital spirit capable of protecting the home and its inhabitants during the cold months. Branches of pine, holly, and ivy could be woven into wreaths to adorn doors and windows or placed on the home altar, serving as an offering to the Mother Goddess.

Light also played an essential role in the Yule celebrations, symbolizing the return of the sun and the strengthening of hope. Lighting candles scattered throughout the house created an atmosphere of warmth and spirituality. The colors of the candles also had specific meanings: red represented energy and rebirth; green referred to nature and growth; gold evoked sunlight and abundance; and white symbolized purity and renewal. For those who had a fireplace, keeping it lit during the solstice night was a way to reinforce this symbolism and invite the light to remain.

The Yule bonfire, known as the Yule Log, was one of the most traditional rituals. A large log was chosen and decorated with ribbons, herbs, and sacred symbols. When it was set on fire, it should burn for 12 days, representing the months of the coming year. If it was not possible to make a bonfire outdoors, an alternative was to use a large candle to symbolize the Yule Log, lighting it with the same intention of renewing the light.

Another fundamental custom was the preparation of a Yule banquet. In a time when abundance was not guaranteed, this celebration served as a moment of thanksgiving for the harvest and the available food. Roasts, pies, dried fruits, nuts, cakes, and breads were served to family and friends, reinforcing the importance of sharing. The participants toasted to the sun, the earth, and the ancestors, expressing their gratitude for the continuity of life.

Yule also marked a period of spiritual renewal, and one of the most significant rituals was that of rebirth. To perform it, everything that needed to be left behind was written on a piece of paper: habits, limiting beliefs, or unwanted situations. This paper was burned in the bonfire or in a candle, representing liberation and detachment. Then, a new paper was written with wishes and intentions for the next cycle. This paper could be kept in a special place or buried in the ground, symbolizing the seed that would germinate in the future.

Meditation on the solstice was a common practice for those who wished to connect more deeply with the energy of Yule. In a quiet environment, they closed their eyes and visualized the sunlight filling their bodies and renewing their strength. This practice allowed not only a moment of introspection but also the opportunity to align with natural cycles.

Expressing gratitude was another pillar of the celebration. Creating a list with everything that had been achieved during the year helped to recognize the blessings received. This list could be read aloud, written in a diary, or placed on an altar of gratitude, reinforcing the importance of recognition and abundance.

Creating a solar symbol was an artistic and spiritual way to mark the occasion. Drawing, painting, or embroidering a sun, or any other symbol that represented light, became an act of devotion. This amulet could be used as part of the decoration or carried with you throughout the year, as a reminder of constant rebirth.

The exchange of gifts, although today associated with Christmas, also had roots in winter festivals. Giving gifts symbolized sharing and the desire for the well-being of others, reinforcing the idea that, even in the darkest periods, generosity and unity should prevail.

Music was an essential part of the festivities, with songs that celebrated light and renewal. Singing joyful melodies or listening to inspiring music helped to create a vibrant atmosphere and connected people to the ancestry of the ritual.

Although many Yule traditions have been incorporated into Christmas, it is possible to rescue and adapt these customs for a more authentic experience of their pagan origins. Even for those who celebrate Christmas, the inclusion of Yule elements allows for a deeper connection with natural cycles.

If there is no fireplace or space for a bonfire, it is possible to adapt the rituals for indoor environments. Candles can replace the ritual fire, and aromatic herbs or incense can be used to create an atmosphere of spirituality and purification.

Yule is a time of renewal, hope, and celebration of light. By connecting with this ancestral energy, it is possible to prepare for the new cycle, strengthen gratitude, and fill life with meaning and joy.

Yule is a time to celebrate life, hope, and the rebirth of light. By connecting with the energy of this sacred night, you can prepare for the new cycle that begins, renew your energies, and bring more light and joy into your life.

Chapter 11
Imbolc
The Purification

Imbolc - pronounced "im-bolk" or "im-molg" - also known as Oimelc or Lady Day, is a Celtic festival that celebrates the awakening of the earth after winter, the first signs of spring, and the promise of renewal. Celebrated on February 1st or 2nd in the northern hemisphere - and on August 1st in the southern hemisphere - Imbolc is a time of purification, inspiration, fertility, and preparation for the new cycle that is approaching.

Imbolc, whose name derives from Gaelic and means "in milk" or "milk of the ewe", carries a deep symbolism linked to the renewal and awakening of life. This designation is due to the fact that, in this period of the year, the ewes begin to produce milk to feed their newborn lambs, one of the first signs of the imminent arrival of spring. This moment represents not only the renewal of the earth, but also a cycle of nourishment and growth, preparing nature and living beings for the abundance that will come with the following season.

In addition to its connection with the natural cycle of animals and the earth, Imbolc is closely associated with the Celtic goddess Brigid, also known as Brighid or

Bride. Revered as a divinity of fire, poetry, healing, metallurgy, and fertility, Brigid is a powerful and multifaceted figure within Celtic mythology. Her presence manifests itself in multiple aspects, being considered a triple goddess, representing the phases of the maiden, mother, and crone. As guardian of the sacred fire, Brigid symbolizes inspiration and transformation, guiding those who seek clarity, creativity, and healing in their lives.

Imbolc, therefore, is a festival dedicated to purification and renewal, a celebration of the return of light and the preparation for the growth that spring will bring. It is a propitious moment to get rid of the old, rekindle the inner flame, and plant the seeds of the future, both in the literal and symbolic sense.

The rituals of Imbolc are ancestral practices that aim to purify the body, mind, spirit, and environment, honor the increasing sunlight, and connect with the inspiring energy of Brigid. One of the most common rituals is spring cleaning, a practice that symbolizes the elimination of stagnant winter energies and the renewal of physical and spiritual spaces. To carry it out, you should start by opening all the windows of the house, allowing fresh air to circulate and carry away any trace of stagnation. Then, each room should be cleaned carefully, removing unnecessary objects and donating or discarding what is no longer useful. During cleaning, it is possible to visualize the heavy and stagnant energy being replaced by a lighter and more invigorating vibration. The use of incense of purifying herbs, such as sage, rosemary, and bay leaf, or the sprinkling of water with salt in the corners of the rooms can enhance this energetic renewal.

In addition to the purification of spaces, it is essential to perform a personal purification ritual, reinforcing the commitment to internal renewal. A ritual bath can be prepared using coarse salt and herbs such as rosemary, lavender, and mint, or essential oils of lemon, orange, and eucalyptus. During the bath, it is important to imagine all physical, emotional, and energetic impurities being dissolved and carried away by the water. To intensify the ritual, white or blue candles can be lit around the environment, symbolizing peace and purification. At the end, wearing clean and light-colored clothes will help seal this feeling of renewal and lightness.

Creating an Imbolc altar is another significant way to honor the energy of this festival and the presence of Brigid. For this, a special space in the house should be chosen and covered with a white, light yellow, or light green cloth. On the altar, traditional symbols of this celebration can be placed, such as an image or statue of Brigid, candles in white, yellow, or green colors, a Brigid's Cross, typical flowers of the season - such as daffodils, primroses and saffron -, seeds or sprouts representing the potential for growth, a container with water symbolizing purification, and a small cauldron, which refers to the womb of the Goddess and the power of transformation. Craft tools, such as balls of wool, needles, paints, or musical instruments, representing the creativity and inspiration that Brigid grants to her devotees, can also be added.

Another essential element of Imbolc is Brigid's Cross, a traditional symbol made with straw, reeds, or other natural materials. This cross has four arms, which represent the elements of nature or the four directions, and an intertwined center, which symbolizes unity and protection. Creating this cross is a meditative and meaningful activity, and, once finished, it can be hung on the door of the house or in a prominent place to attract blessings and protection to the home and its inhabitants.

As goddess of fire, Brigid is also honored through the ritual of the sacred flame. Lighting a white candle on the altar or in a special place in the house represents the awakening of the inner light and the strengthening of creativity, hope, and inspiration. During this ritual, it is recommended to meditate observing the flame, visualizing it as the divine spark within you, and ask Brigid to illuminate the paths and bring clarity and renewal to your life. Reciting a prayer, composing a poem, or singing a song in her honor are additional ways to strengthen this spiritual connection.

The act of planting seeds during Imbolc symbolizes both the beginning of a new cycle and the manifestation of desires and intentions. You can choose seeds of flowers, herbs, or vegetables and plant them in pots or directly in the ground, focusing on visualizing your dreams and projects coming true as the plants grow and bloom. Writing your wishes on small pieces of paper and burying them along with the seeds is a symbolic gesture that reinforces this intention.

Creativity also has a central role in this festival, since Brigid is the patroness of the arts. Reserving a moment to express yourself artistically - whether through writing, painting, music, dance, or crafts - is a way to honor the inspiring energy of this goddess and strengthen the connection with your own creative essence.

Divination is another practice associated with Imbolc, as this is a propitious time to seek insights about the future and clarify paths. Methods such as Tarot, runes, Ogham, or coffee grounds reading can be used to receive messages and guidance. Before starting any reading, you can ask Brigid to illuminate your intuition and bring clear and inspiring answers.

No celebration would be complete without a symbolic banquet, and Imbolc is no exception. Preparing and sharing traditional foods of this time, such as dairy products - milk, cheese, yogurt -, breads, cakes, fruits, and seeds, is a way to celebrate the fertility of the earth and the abundance that is to come. A toast can be made in honor of Brigid, nature, and the ancestors, strengthening the feeling of gratitude and connection.

Finally, a walk at sunrise can be a special moment of introspection and renewal. If the weather permits, going outdoors before the sun rises on the horizon and watching the light take over the sky is a way to connect with the awakening of the earth and feel the vibrant energy of change.

Although Imbolc has ancestral roots, it can be adapted to modern life and individual beliefs. If it is not possible to plant seeds outdoors, they can be grown in pots indoors. If the connection with the goddess Brigid does not make sense to someone, it is possible to honor the feminine energy and creativity in other ways. The most important thing is the intention to align with the natural cycles, purify life, and prepare for the new cycle with an open and light-filled heart.

Imbolc is a time of hope, renewal, and inspiration. By celebrating this festival, you can align yourself with the rhythms of nature, awaken your creativity, and bring more light and joy to your life.

Chapter 12
Ostara
The Spring Equinox

Ostara, also known as the Spring Equinox, is a Celtic festival that celebrates the return of balance between light and darkness, the awakening of nature, the fertility of the earth, and the beginning of the growing season. Celebrated around March 21st in the Northern Hemisphere -and September 21st in the Southern Hemisphere-, Ostara is a time of joy, renewal, new beginnings, and celebration of life.

The name "Ostara" has its roots in the ancient Germanic goddess Eostre, also known as Ostara, a deity associated with spring, fertility, and rebirth. Her figure symbolizes dawn and renewal, representing the promise of longer and more fertile days after the harshness of winter. Among her main symbols, the hare stands out, which symbolizes fertility and agility, and the eggs, representations of the potential and new life that emerges with the arrival of the season.

The Spring Equinox marks a unique moment in the cycle of nature, in which light and darkness meet in perfect balance. This astronomical phenomenon occurs when day and night have exactly the same duration, a milestone that marks the transition to progressively longer and sunnier days. For the Celtic peoples, this was a period of great celebration, as it meant the return of life to the land after months of cold and scarcity. The germination of seeds, the flowering of plants, and the reproduction of animals were visible signs of this renewal, and the rituals of Ostara reflected this deep connection with natural cycles.

The celebration of Ostara involves a series of rituals that honor both the balance between light and darkness and the fertility of the earth and the promise of growth. Among the most common practices is the decoration of spaces with symbols of spring. For this, the use of vibrant colors, such as green, yellow, pink, light blue, and white, which evoke the energy of renewal, is recommended. The house can be adorned with typical seasonal flowers, such as daffodils, tulips, hyacinths, primroses, and violets, bringing beauty and fragrance to the environment. Painted or decorated eggs play an important role in this context, functioning as symbols of fertility and new life. It is possible to personalize them with Celtic symbols, vibrant colors, or drawings that represent wishes and intentions for the new cycle. In addition, images or statues of hares and rabbits can be displayed in the space, reinforcing the fertile symbology of Ostara. Colored fabrics, ribbons, and various ornaments help to create a festive and harmonious environment.

Another essential practice for the celebration of the festival is the creation of an altar dedicated to the goddess Eostre and the energies of spring. This altar can be set up in any special space in the house, being covered with green, yellow, or white fabrics, which symbolize the rebirth of nature. Among the items that can be placed on the altar, an image or statue of the goddess, candles in vibrant tones, fresh flowers, decorated eggs, seeds and sprouts, as well as a container with water, representing fertility, stand out. Crystals such as rose quartz, amethyst, citrine, and green quartz can be added to intensify the energy of renewal and balance.

The search for balance is one of the main themes of Ostara, and a simple but powerful ritual can be performed to harmonize internal energies. For this, two candles are lit on the altar: one representing light and the other symbolizing darkness. During the ritual, it is important to meditate on the areas of life in which one feels balanced and those that need adjustments. The visualization of light and darkness integrating within oneself can help in this process, promoting a state of harmony and clarity. To finish, one can recite a prayer, a poem, or even sing a song in homage to balance.

The planting of seeds is also an essential practice of this period, both in a literal and metaphorical sense. The act of sowing flowers, herbs, or vegetables symbolizes the cultivation of new projects and intentions for the future. When planting, it is possible to visualize the wishes for the new cycle growing along with the plants, and a way to reinforce this symbolism is to write intentions on small pieces of paper and bury them together with the seeds.

Another traditional custom that has spanned centuries is the egg hunt, a practice that was later incorporated into the celebrations of Christian Easter. This activity, in addition to being fun, carries a deep symbolism: it represents the search for fertility, for abundance, and for joy. To carry it out, painted or decorated eggs can be hidden around the house or garden, inviting friends and family to participate. Small gifts or messages can be placed inside the eggs, making the experience even more special.

Taking advantage of the arrival of spring outdoors is an excellent way to connect with the energy of the season. A picnic in a park, forest, or garden allows you to enjoy the beauty of nature while sharing fresh and light foods, such as salads, fruits, sandwiches, and juices. This moment can be an opportunity to celebrate friendship, life, and rebirth, while enjoying the sun and fresh air.

Another way to honor Ostara is through conscious walks in nature. Carefully observing the flowers blooming, the birds singing, and the animals in activity allows for a deeper connection with the energy of spring. Feeling the earth under your feet, breathing in the scent of the flowers, and absorbing the sunlight are practices that revitalize body and spirit.

As a form of gratitude to nature, an offering ritual can be performed. Small gifts, such as flowers, seeds, fruits, honey, or milk, can be left in a special place, such as the base of a tree, near a river, or on a rock. This gesture symbolizes recognition and respect for natural cycles and the abundance that the earth offers.

Dancing and singing are spontaneous expressions of joy and vitality, and during Ostara, these practices can be incorporated into the celebrations. Joyful music can be played, encouraging free and spontaneous movements, which help to awaken vital energy. Singing songs that exalt spring and renewal also strengthens the connection with the essence of the festival.

Energetic cleansing is another important aspect of this period of renewal. Just as a physical cleaning is done in the house, removing stagnant energies from the environment and from one's own energetic field can bring significant benefits. This can be done through the use of incense, herb baths, or fumigation with sage, promoting an atmosphere of freshness and lightness.

Ostara, although it has ancestral roots, can be easily adapted to modern life and individual beliefs. For those who live in small spaces, such as apartments, it is possible to grow plants in pots or create a small vertical garden. If the connection with the figure of the goddess Eostre is not natural, it is possible to focus on the general energy of spring and the symbolic renewal that this time of year brings.

Many of the traditional elements of Ostara were assimilated by the celebrations of Christian Easter, such as decorated eggs, rabbits, and flowers. For those who celebrate this date, there are subtle ways to integrate pagan meanings into the festivity, rescuing the ancestral origins of this celebration. The essential thing is to recognize and honor the energy of renewal, balance, and fertility that permeates this time of year, allowing this force to guide new beginnings and awaken the joy of life blossoming again.

Ostara is a time to celebrate the rebirth of life, balance, and fertility. By connecting with the energy of this time of year, you can renew your energies, plant the seeds for the future, and bring more joy and abundance to your life.

Chapter 13
Beltane
The Sacred Fire

Beltane - pronounced "bel-tain" or "bee-al-ti-na" - also known as May Day or Cétshamhain, is a Celtic festival that celebrates the height of spring, the union of masculine and feminine, the fertility of the earth, and the power of fire. Celebrated on May 1st in the northern hemisphere - and November 1st in the southern hemisphere - Beltane is a time of passion, joy, creativity, and celebration of life in its fullness.

Beltane, whose pronunciation can vary between "bel-tain" and "bee-al-ti-na," has deep roots in Celtic culture and symbolizes the vibrant transition from spring to the peak of its strength, marking the fertility of the earth and the potency of sacred fire. The word "Beltane" comes from Gaelic and means "bright fire" or "fire of Bel," a reference to the Celtic god Belenos, associated with the sun, light, and healing. Fire, moreover, occupies a central role in this festival, representing ardent passion, vital energy, purification, and renewal.

The celebration takes place at the midpoint between the spring equinox and the summer solstice, when nature displays its fullness, the fields bloom, the animals mate, and the energy of life pulsates intensely.

For the Celtic peoples, Beltane was an occasion to honor the sacred union between the masculine and feminine principle, ensuring the continuity of life and the prosperity of the earth. The rituals were vibrant, full of dances, bonfires, and festivities that exalted fertility and connection with the sacred.

Among the traditional customs, the burning of Beltane bonfires was one of the most important. They were lit on hilltops and in sacred places, where people gathered to celebrate. If there is no possibility of making a bonfire outdoors, candles can be used as a representation of the sacred fire. Lighting red, orange, yellow, or gold candles creates a symbolic atmosphere of warmth and transformation. In ancient times, it was believed that jumping over the flames of the bonfire promoted purification, renewal, and attracted luck and fertility. Today, this practice can be adapted with candles or even with the visualization of this ritual in a meditation.

Another iconic element of Beltane is the dance around the Maypole, a phallic symbol that represents the union of the God and Goddess. Colored ribbons are woven around the pole by dancers, creating an intertwined pattern that symbolizes fertility and the interconnection of all things. If a traditional Maypole is not available, any pole, tree, or even a tall candle can serve as a substitute for this ritualistic dance.

In addition to dances and fire, rituals of sacred union are an essential part of the celebration. For couples, this is a perfect time to reaffirm vows, light candles together, exchange symbolic gifts, and share a special meal. For singles, Beltane offers the opportunity to harmonize the masculine and feminine energies within themselves, recognizing and balancing qualities such as strength and sensitivity, logic and intuition.

The decoration also plays an important role in the festivities. The house can be adorned with spring flowers, such as roses, daisies, lilies, and wildflowers, and green branches of trees such as willow, ash, and hawthorn can be used to embellish doors and windows. Floral crowns and garlands are an excellent way to bring the vibrant energy of the season into the home environment.

For those who want an even deeper connection, creating an altar dedicated to Beltane can be a powerful practice. This altar can be set up in a special space in the house, covered with a fabric in the colors of the season - red, orange, green or floral - and decorated with symbolic elements such as images of divinities of love and fertility, colored candles, flowers, crystals such as rose quartz and garnet, fruits such as strawberries and pomegranates and even a chalice with wine, representing the feminine principle, next to a wand or athame, representing the masculine principle.

For those seeking fertility in any aspect - whether in the conception of a child, in the realization of projects or in the flowering of creativity -, a specific ritual can be performed. This ritual may include prayers to the divinities of fertility, the use of symbolic herbs and crystals, and even an intimate ceremony of consecration of the desire. For those who do not seek literal fertility, Beltane can be an excellent time to celebrate the abundance of life and the infinite capacity for creation and manifestation of dreams.

Food is also a fundamental part of the celebration. The table can be filled with symbolic foods, such as red fruits, cherries, pomegranates, honey, milk, breads, cakes, and wine. Sharing this meal with friends and family strengthens bonds, promoting an environment of joy and connection. In addition, a toast can be made in honor of the gods of fertility, the earth, and the ancestors, celebrating the vibrant energy of the season.

Another significant ritual is that of purification with fire. For this, one can write on a piece of paper all that one wishes to release - fears, limiting beliefs, resentments or negative habits - and burn it in the bonfire or in a candle, visualizing these energies being transformed into ashes and dissipated by the wind. This act symbolizes renewal, allowing the new to enter our lives with more lightness and harmony.

For those who want an even greater immersion, spending the night of Beltane outdoors can be a transformative experience. In some Celtic traditions, sleeping under the stars on this night was a way to connect deeply with the energy of nature and with the spirits of the earth. If there is a safe space available, this can be a magical opportunity to meditate, observe the sky, sing, and celebrate the arrival of summer.

Finally, one of the most simple and enchanting traditions of Beltane involves the morning dew. It is believed that this dew has magical and healing properties, especially for beauty and youth. At dawn, one can collect some of this dew and use it to wash the face, bless objects, or incorporate it into spells and rituals of renewal.

Even in modern life, Beltane can be celebrated in an adapted way, without losing its essence. In urban environments, candles can replace bonfires, incense can be used to purify spaces, and small altars can be set up on tables or shelves. The important thing is the intention to honor the cycle of life, passion, and fertility, celebrating the vibrant energy that this festival brings.

Regardless of how one chooses to celebrate, Beltane is an invitation to rekindle the inner flame, awaken creativity and cultivate joy and abundance in all aspects of life.

Beltane is a time to celebrate passion, joy, union, and fertility. By connecting with the energy of this festival, you can ignite your inner flame, awaken your creativity and bring more love and abundance to your life.

Chapter 14
Litha
The Summer Solstice

Litha, also known as the Summer Solstice, Midsummer or Alban Hefin, is a Celtic festival that celebrates the peak of the sun's power, the longest day of the year and the abundance of nature. Celebrated around June 21st in the northern hemisphere -and December 21st in the southern hemisphere-, Litha is a time of strength, vitality, joy, gratitude and celebration of light.

The Summer Solstice is a special astronomical moment, marking the instant when the sun reaches its highest point in the sky, resulting in the longest day and the shortest night of the year. From this peak of light, the days begin to gradually shorten, announcing the transition to the second half of the solar cycle. However, even with the decrease in daylight hours, the sun's energy remains intense and abundant, radiating strength and vitality.

For the Celts, this period was a sacred moment of honor to the Sun God, recognized as the primordial source of life and energy. Litha was celebrated as a time of jubilation, when the fertility of the earth, the fullness of nature and the generosity of future harvests were exalted. The festival was also an opportunity to reaffirm the connection with the natural world, perceiving the beauty around and expressing gratitude for the blessings granted. The sun, in this context, was seen not only as a celestial body, but as a symbol of renewal and vital force, which warms, illuminates and sustains all existence.

The rituals performed during Litha are deeply linked to the energy of the sun and the celebration of abundance. These practices aim to honor the light, strengthen personal vitality and promote spiritual connection with the season. There are several ways to celebrate this festival, each carrying a special meaning and providing a moment of introspection and communion with nature.

Watching the sunrise or sunset is one of the simplest and most powerful ways to connect with the essence of Litha. This is a time to contemplate the greatness of the sun, feeling its warmth on the skin and absorbing its revitalizing energy. For this, one can wake up before dawn and find a quiet place to watch the spectacle of the sunrise, observing the subtle changes of color in the sky and feeling the energetic renewal brought by the new day. Similarly, at dusk, it is possible to find a special space to contemplate the sunset, thanking for the light received throughout the day and reflecting on its symbology. During this experience, many people recite prayers, declaim poems or sing songs dedicated to the sun, expressing their gratitude and respect for its constant presence.

Another traditional Litha ritual is the bonfire, one of the central elements of the celebration. Fire represents the strength of the sun and its ability to illuminate and transform. If there is a safe space outdoors, a bonfire can be lit at sunset, gathering around it to sing, dance, meditate or share stories. Throwing aromatic herbs such as rosemary, sage, laurel, chamomile or lavender into the flames intensifies the experience, releasing purifying fragrances into the air. This practice can be accompanied by a symbolic visualization, imagining that the fire consumes and dissipates negative energies, opening the way to light, joy and renewal. For those who cannot make a bonfire, the use of candles in shades of yellow, orange or gold can replace this element, keeping alive the symbology of the sacred flame.

Creating an altar dedicated to Litha is also a powerful way to channel the energy of the festival. This space can be set up anywhere special inside the house, decorated with vibrant colors such as yellow, orange, gold or white. Among the elements that can compose this altar, there are images or statues of solar divinities, such as Apollo, Ra, Lugh or Belenos, in addition to colored candles, seasonal flowers—sunflowers, daisies, calendulas and lilies—, fresh fruits such as peaches, apricots, melons and mangoes, and energetic crystals such as citrine, amber, tiger's eye and pyrite. Symbolic objects linked to the sun, such as spirals and solar disks, can also be included to strengthen the connection with this energy.

An essential moment within the Litha celebration is the gratitude ritual. This festival is an opportunity to reflect on the blessings received and express appreciation for them. For this, one can create a list with everything there is to thank for in life, whether writing in a diary, making an offering to nature or simply verbalizing this gratitude. Some people prefer to set up a specific altar for this purpose, while others opt for a sincere prayer directed to the Sun God, Mother Earth or ancestors, recognizing their gifts and asking for continuity for the cycle of abundance.

The cuisine plays a significant role in the Litha festivities, being a delicious and symbolic way to honor the occasion. Preparing a special meal with seasonal ingredients—such as fresh fruits, colorful salads, artisan breads, sweet cakes and honey—is a way to bring the energy of the earth to the moment of celebration. Sharing this food with friends and family strengthens affective bonds and reinforces the spirit of joy and abundance characteristic of this period. Many traditions include toasts to the sun and nature, using symbolic drinks such as mead or natural juices.

Being outdoors and walking in nature is also an excellent way to connect with the vibrant energy of the solstice. A conscious walk through a park, forest or beach allows you to observe the fullness of life around, feel the strength of the earth under your feet and perceive the natural cycles that govern the world. During this walk, you can dedicate a moment to observe the animals, touch the plants and express gratitude for the generosity of Mother Earth.

Sunbathing, when done consciously and respecting the limits of the body, can be a true ritual of energetic recharge. By exposing yourself to the sun, it is possible to visualize its light penetrating each cell, nourishing and revitalizing the entire being. This is a powerful exercise of absorption of solar energy, but it must be done with caution, using adequate protection and avoiding times of high solar intensity.

The practice with crystals is also quite associated with Litha, being possible to work with stones such as citrine, tiger's eye and amber to enhance the connection with the sun. These crystals can be carried with you, placed on the altar or used in meditations and energizing rituals.

In addition, Litha is a propitious period for rituals of healing, both physical and emotional. Using candles, incense and herbs in wellness rituals can help in the renewal of energies and in the restoration of balance. During these moments, one can visualize the light of the sun penetrating the points that need healing, promoting restoration and strengthening.

Finally, creativity is encouraged in this festival. Creating art—whether through painting, writing, dance or music—is a way to channel the inspiring energy of Litha and express feelings and intentions. This is a time of celebration of life in its fullness, and any artistic manifestation can be a powerful way to honor this date.

Even in the modern world, it is possible to adapt the traditions of Litha to different realities and personal beliefs. Those who live in apartments can set up small altars, use candles and incense to represent the fire, and decorate the space with flowers and fruits of the season. Similarly, those who do not worship specific divinities can simply direct their celebration to the energy of the sun and light, recognizing their influence on all living beings.

Litha invites us to celebrate strength, vitality and abundance, reminding us that light is always present, even in the moments when we begin to walk towards darkness. By connecting with this festival, we can strengthen our own energy, thank for what we have already received and prepare ourselves for the next cycles of the Wheel of the Year.

Litha is a time to celebrate strength, vitality, joy and abundance. By connecting with the energy of this festival, you can strengthen your vital energy, thank for the blessings received and prepare yourself for the next cycle of the wheel of the year.

Chapter 15
Lughnasadh
The First Harvest

Lughnasadh - pronounced "loo-nah-sah" - or Lammas, is a Celtic festival that celebrates the first harvest, the beginning of the harvest season, and the generosity of the earth. Celebrated on August 1st in the Northern Hemisphere - and February 1st or 2nd in the Southern Hemisphere - Lughnasadh is a time of gratitude, acknowledgment, sacrifice, and preparation for the future.

Lughnasadh, whose name means "celebration of Lugh" or "games of Lugh," is a celebration in honor of the Celtic god Lugh, a deity associated with light, skills, arts, war, and royalty. Lugh was a master of many art forms, a skilled warrior, and a just leader, revered by the Celts as one of the most important gods in their pantheon. Legend has it that Lugh instituted the Lughnasadh games as a tribute to his adoptive mother, Tailtiu, who dedicated her life to making the lands fertile for agriculture and, as a result of her hard work, died of exhaustion. To honor her sacrifice, Lugh organized festivals that included athletic competitions, horse races, fairs, markets, and celebrations, bringing people together for moments of gratitude and recognition of the abundance that the land provided them.

This festival occurs at the midpoint between the summer solstice and the autumn equinox, a time when the first grains are harvested, the fruits reach their maturity, and nature begins its transition to the decline of the year. For the Celts, Lughnasadh was not only a celebration of abundance but also a time of reflection on the need to preserve resources and prepare for the approaching winter. The recognition of the cycle of life, death, and rebirth was central to this culture, and this festival symbolized the interdependence between sacrifice and the continuity of life.

The rituals performed during this period are focused on gratitude for the harvest, connection with the earth, and preparation for future challenges. One of the most symbolic rituals is the making of Lughnasadh Bread, known as "Lammas Bread." The bread represents the harvested grain and the nourishment that sustains life, becoming one of the central elements of the celebration. To make it, you can use wheat, rye, barley, or other grains, adding seeds, herbs, or dried fruits to enrich its flavor and symbolism. During preparation, while the dough is kneaded, it is recommended to visualize the energy of the earth and the sun uniting with the dough, blessing it with abundance and nourishment. The bread should be baked with intention and love, and later shared with family and friends as a gesture of celebration and communion.

Another significant ritual is the creation of an altar dedicated to Lughnasadh and the god Lugh. This altar can be set up in a special place in the house, covered with a fabric in warm tones, such as yellow, orange, gold, or brown, representing the energy of the sun and the harvest. On it, you can place symbols related to the festival, such as images or statues of Lugh and other harvest deities, candles in golden tones, bundles of wheat and barley, seasonal fruits such as apples, pears, blackberries, and plums, breads and cakes prepared with grains, miniature agricultural tools, such as scythes and plows, as well as symbols associated with Lugh, such as spears and solar disks.

Gratitude is one of the most important aspects of this festival, and a gratitude ritual can be performed to recognize the blessings received. This can be done by writing a list containing all the positive things in life: health, relationships, achievements, and lessons learned. Expressing this gratitude can occur in various ways, such as verbalizing thanks, writing in a journal, lighting candles on the altar, or making an offering to nature as a form of return.

Offering something to nature is a gesture of acknowledgment of the generosity of the earth. For this, it is possible to leave food such as bread, fruits, grains, honey, milk, or water in a special natural place, such as the base of a tree, on the banks of a river, or on a rock. Before making the offering, it is essential to ask permission from nature, demonstrating respect, and end the ritual with a sincere thank you.

The celebration also involves sharing food and drinks. Preparing a special meal using typical ingredients of the season, such as corn, pumpkin, potato, tomato, and red fruits, is a way to honor the harvest. The food should be shared in a moment of celebration with family and friends, and a toast can be made in honor of Lugh, the earth, and all living beings.

One of the most profound rituals of this festival is the symbolic sacrifice ritual, which represents the necessary exchange for growth and the continuity of life. Just as grains need to be cut to become bread, certain aspects of life need to be left behind so that new cycles can begin. This ritual can be performed by choosing an object, a talent, a habit, or any element that represents something you want to abandon in exchange for something new. Writing on a paper what you want to sacrifice and what you expect to receive in return is a way to concretize this intention. The paper can be burned in a bonfire or candle flame, symbolizing transformation and renewal.

Games and competitions are also part of the tradition of Lughnasadh, harking back to the ancient games instituted by Lugh. To honor this spirit, it is possible to organize activities such as races, tug of war, weightlifting, or even board games, encouraging fun and celebration of vitality.

Divination is another element that can be incorporated into the celebrations. As Lughnasadh marks the transition between seasons, this is a propitious time to seek guidance about the future. Methods such as Tarot, runes, Ogham, or reading coffee grounds can be used to access messages and insights, asking Lugh to illuminate intuition and bring clarity about the paths to follow.

In addition to traditional rituals, artistic and artisanal expression is encouraged during Lughnasadh, as Lugh is the god of skills and arts. Dedicating oneself to creative activities, such as weaving straw, making corn dolls, sculpting, painting, or weaving, is a way to honor the energy of this god and strengthen individual abilities.

Finally, walking through a field of grains, if there is a possibility, is a powerful way to connect with the essence of the festival. Feeling the presence of nature, touching the ripe grains, and expressing gratitude directly to the earth strengthens the bond with natural cycles and reinforces the purpose of this harvest period.

Currently, Lughnasadh can be adapted to modern life in various ways. Those who live in urban areas can create small altars at home, use candles to represent fire, and decorate their spaces with fruits, breads, and flowers of the season. For those who do not identify with the figure of Lugh, the festival can be celebrated focusing on the energy of the harvest, gratitude, and sacrifice in a more comprehensive way. The essential thing is the intention to connect with this cycle and celebrate the abundance of life.

Thus, Lughnasadh remains a period of reverence to the generosity of the earth, of recognition of the sacrifice necessary for continuity, and of preparation for the new cycles to come. By experiencing this celebration, it is possible to strengthen the connection with nature, recognize one's own achievements, and consciously prepare for the challenges and blessings of the future.

Lughnasadh is a time to celebrate the harvest, thank for the generosity of the earth, recognize the sacrifice necessary for growth, and prepare for the future. By connecting with the energy of this festival, you can strengthen your connection with nature, celebrate your successes, and prepare for the next cycle of the wheel of the year.

Chapter 16
Mabon
The Autumn Equinox

Mabon, also known as the Autumn Equinox, Second Harvest, or Alban Elfed, is a Celtic festival that celebrates the balance between light and darkness, the final harvest, gratitude for the blessings received, and preparation for winter. Celebrated around September 21st in the northern hemisphere -and March 21st in the southern hemisphere-, Mabon is a time of introspection, reflection, thanksgiving, and planning.

The name "Mabon" has a relatively recent origin, having been coined by Aidan Kelly in the 1970s. He was inspired by Mabon ap Modron, a character from Welsh mythology, son of the goddess Modron, the Great Mother. Although there is no concrete evidence that the ancient Celts used this name for the autumn equinox, the term quickly became popular in the modern pagan community, becoming a widely accepted reference for this time of year.

The Autumn Equinox is a special moment in the astronomical calendar, marking the perfect balance between day and night, when both parts have the same duration. This phenomenon occurs because the sun crosses the celestial equator, and, from that point on, the days begin to shorten, while the nights become longer. This event symbolizes the decline of the sun and the transition to winter, a period of recollection, introspection and preparation for the challenges that the cold months will bring.

For the Celtic peoples, Mabon represented the second harvest of the year, a crucial moment to ensure survival during the winter. At this stage, fruits such as apples, grapes and pomegranates, as well as nuts and vegetables, were harvested and stored. It was a time of deep gratitude for the abundance of the land and for the guaranteed sustenance for the months of scarcity that would come. In addition to the practical issue of the harvest, this celebration brought a significant spiritual dimension, as it symbolized the duality of existence: light and darkness, joy and sadness, growth and decline. Thus, Mabon was also a period of reflection and search for inner harmony, inviting people to find balance in their own lives.

Mabon rituals are focused on celebrating this balance and expressing gratitude for the gifts received throughout the year. Several practices can be incorporated to make this celebration special and meaningful. Creating an altar for Mabon is a powerful way to honor this energy and connect with the spirit of the season. To do this, choose a special place in your home and cover it with a fabric that represents autumn, in shades of brown, orange, red, gold or purple. On the altar, arrange symbols of the harvest, such as dried leaves in vibrant colors, seasonal fruits -apples, grapes, pomegranates, pears and pumpkins-, as well as nuts, chestnuts and seeds. Ears of corn and wheat are also important symbolic elements, as are candles in the colors of autumn. Crystals associated with this time, such as amber, citrine, tiger's eye, carnelian and red jasper, can be placed to enhance the energy. For those who worship deities, images or statues of gods and goddesses linked to the harvest and the underworld, such as Demeter, Persephone, Dionysus, Hades, Cernunnos and the Mother Goddess, can be incorporated into the altar.

Expressing gratitude is an essential practice during Mabon. Take a moment to reflect on all the blessings received during the year and write a list containing everything that brought you happiness and learning: health, family, friends, work, achievements and even challenges that provided growth. After this reflection, read the list aloud, record it in a journal or offer a symbolic gift to nature, as a form of thanksgiving. A prayer or supplication directed to the gods and goddesses of the harvest, to Mother Earth or to the ancestors can also be made to reinforce this energy of gratitude.

Mabon also invites the search for balance. To symbolize this harmony, light two candles on the altar, one representing light and the other representing darkness. During this moment, meditate on your own life and identify where there is balance and where adjustments are needed. Visualize the energies of day and night harmonizing within you, promoting a state of peace and integration. You can complement this ritual by composing or reciting a poem, singing a song or simply remaining in silence, absorbing the energy of the moment.

Connecting with nature is another powerful way to celebrate Mabon. Take a walk outdoors, observing the transformations of the season. In a park, forest or any natural environment, contemplate the falling leaves, the warm tones of the trees and the signs of the fauna's preparation for winter. Breathe deeply, absorb the energy of the earth and express your gratitude for the beauty and abundance of the natural world.

Preparing a meal with typical seasonal foods is also a delicious way to honor this festival. Cooking dishes with pumpkin, sweet potato, apples, pears, grapes, nuts and chestnuts brings the flavor and essence of autumn to the celebration. Roasts, breads and hot dishes can be shared with family and friends in a special banquet, strengthening bonds and community energy. A toast to the gods and goddesses of the harvest, the earth and future prosperity can conclude this festive moment.

Another significant Mabon ritual is that of release. Just as trees drop their leaves, this is a time to let go of what no longer serves you. Take a piece of paper and write down everything you want to leave behind: fears, worries, hurts, resentments, harmful habits or limiting patterns. Then, burn this paper in a candle or bonfire, visualizing the transformation of these negative energies into ashes, being carried away by the wind. This symbolic act helps create space for the new and promotes a sense of renewal and lightness.

Bringing the essence of autumn into your home through decoration is also a simple and powerful way to celebrate Mabon. Use warm colors and natural elements, such as dried leaves, branches, pinecones, pumpkins and fruits, to create a cozy and attuned environment with the season.

Introspection is also an essential aspect of this festival. Set aside time to reflect on the cycle that is closing, recording your experiences, learnings and challenges in a journal. Meditating, reading an inspiring book or simply being in silence can help process this moment of transition and establish intentions for the next cycle.

Honoring ancestors is another valuable practice of Mabon. Creating a small altar with photos and objects that refer to those who came before us, lighting candles or offering food and flowers are ways to demonstrate respect and connection. Visiting a cemetery, making a prayer or simply remembering with affection the stories and teachings transmitted by them strengthens this spiritual bond.

Finally, preparing for winter is a practical and symbolic action. Organizing the house, cleaning spaces, storing food and planning the cold months that will come are ways to align with the natural cycle of the earth. Just as nature withdraws, we can also prepare ourselves for moments of greater recollection and reflection.

Although Mabon is an ancestral celebration, its essence can be easily adapted to modern life. For those who live in small spaces, a simple altar on a shelf or table is enough to create a focal point of connection. If devotion to Celtic deities does not resonate with your beliefs, it is possible to direct the energy of the celebration to thank nature, the universe or simply the cycle of life itself. The important thing is the intention: to recognize and honor the balance, the harvest and the transition that this period represents.

Mabon is an invitation to celebrate harmony, gratitude and renewal. By connecting with this energy, we reflect on our journey, leave behind what no longer serves us and prepare ourselves for the new challenges and opportunities that the next cycle will bring.

Mabon is a time to celebrate balance, gratitude, harvest and preparation for winter. By connecting with the energy of this festival, you can reflect on your life, release what no longer serves you, thank for the blessings received and prepare for the next cycle of the wheel of the year.

Part III
Rites of Passage and Celebrations

Chapter 17
Birth and Naming

In Celtic tradition, the birth of a child was a sacred event, a moment of great joy and celebration, but also of care and protection. It was believed that the newborn was especially vulnerable to the forces of the Otherworld, and therefore, rituals were performed to ensure their safety, health, and connection with the community and the gods.

Immediately after birth, the child was welcomed into an environment carefully prepared to protect them from negative influences and ensure that their arrival into the world was blessed by good energies. The first ritual performed was the purifying bath, a practice loaded with symbolism and sacred intentions. The water, an essential element of life, was enriched with herbs of protective and healing power, such as rosemary, sage, rue, and vervain. Each of these herbs had a special meaning: rosemary brought strength and clarity, sage promoted wisdom and warded off evil spirits, rue protected against envy and dense energies, and vervain was a channel of blessings and purification. The child was gently bathed in this warm infusion, while prayers were murmured to ensure that they began their journey in life free from any evil influence.

Next, the environment where mother and child were located was purified through smoking, an ancestral ritual that used the smoke of sacred herbs to cleanse and protect the space. Branches of sage, cedar, and juniper were burned slowly, and the smoke was guided by the hands of the elders around the cradle and the doors and windows, forming an invisible shield against unwanted spirits. The deep aroma of these herbs, in addition to warding off negative energies, brought a sense of tranquility and connection with the spiritual world.

Another fundamental aspect of protecting the newborn was the use of amulets, material symbols of strength and protection. In the cradle or on the child's clothing, small natural objects were placed with the intention of ensuring safety and luck. Protective stones, such as amethyst or tiger's eye, could be discreetly sewn into a small linen bag. Shells, collected by the rivers and oceans, represented the harmony and fluidity of life. Branches of sacred trees, such as holly and yew, were placed near the child to channel the energy of the ancestors and the earth. In addition, Celtic symbols such as the triskle, which represented the cycles of life, and the triquetra, which evoked balance and connection with divine forces, were engraved on small pieces of wood and placed next to the cradle.

One of the simplest, yet profoundly effective gestures, was tying a red thread on the baby's wrist or ankle. In many Celtic traditions, red was the color of protection, capable of deflecting the evil eye and keeping the child safe from unwanted influences. This thread was often blessed by an elder or a druid, who murmured words of strength and health before gently tying it on the child's skin.

Words, in turn, possessed immense power. Thus, prayers and incantations were recited by family members and members of the community to envelop the child in an aura of blessings. Parents invoked the protection of the gods, asked for health and prosperity, and offered their vows of love and commitment. Each member present could also recite positive wishes for the baby, reinforcing the connection between the new life and their community.

After this initial protection phase, the time came to integrate the child into the world around them. The presentation of the baby was not just a symbolic act; it was an essential step for them to be recognized by both humans and natural elements. On full moon nights, some families took their children outside, gently lifting them towards the sky so that the silver light bathed their skin. The moon, a symbol of intuition and the cycles of life, was seen as a guardian of the child's soul, granting its protection and wisdom.

Other traditions performed the presentation to the sun at dawn, allowing the first rays to illuminate the child and fill their being with vital energy. The sun, associated with strength and renewal, bestowed its blessing upon them, ensuring vigor and healthy growth.

In addition to the stars, the four elements were also honored in this ritual. The child could be gently touched with a stone, representing the earth and its stability; a feather, symbolizing the air and intelligence; a lit candle, evoking fire and its transforming energy; and drops of water, ensuring fluidity and balanced emotion. In some cases, the baby was taken to a place where all these elements were present: a forest near a river, where the wind blew gently and a fire burned, symbolizing the connection with all the forces that made up existence.

The presentation to the tribe was, finally, a moment of celebration and welcome. The members of the community gathered to receive the new member with joy, promises of protection, and vows of happiness. The older women murmured advice and prayers, the men uttered words of courage and strength, and the older children gently touched the baby, establishing bonds from an early age. This moment not only strengthened the child's sense of belonging but also reaffirmed the bonds between the members of the tribe.

The culmination of this cycle of rituals was the moment of naming, an event of great importance. The chosen name was not just a label; it was a link between the child, their ancestors, and their destiny. In some families, the name was given soon after birth, while in others a period was awaited until the child showed traits of their personality. This name could be inspired by various sources: their appearance, such as "Ruadh" for a child with reddish hair; a beloved ancestor, perpetuating the lineage; a protective deity, such as Brigid for a girl blessed by creativity and healing; or even a sacred animal, such as Cuán, "little wolf," for a strong and agile boy.

The naming ceremony gathered the community around the baby, in an environment charged with spirituality. Druids or elders were called upon to invoke the presence of the gods and bless the child. The name was then proclaimed aloud, allowing both those present and the spirits to hear and recognize the identity of that being. As an offering, food, drinks, and flowers were placed on an altar, symbolizing gratitude and welcome. Parents and godparents, if any, touched the child and whispered words of protection and promises to guide them on their journey.

The naming ritual culminated in a vibrant celebration, full of food, music, and dance. The birth and name of a new life were seen as events worthy of joy, and the party served to reinforce the union between all. Laughter echoed, songs were sung, and stories of ancestors were recalled, connecting the past to the future.

Today, these rituals can be adapted to reflect our beliefs and lifestyles. We can still perform purifying baths, use amulets, recite blessings, and present our children to nature and the community. The choice of name can be made with intention and meaning, honoring our roots and desires for the child. We can create personalized ceremonies, inviting loved ones to witness this special moment, exchange vows, and celebrate together. The essential thing is that the ritual is a reflection of love, connection, and the desire for a prosperous future for the new life that has just arrived.

    The important thing is to create a ritual that is meaningful for us and our family, that celebrates the arrival of the new life, that connects them with their roots, and that blesses them with love, protection, and wisdom.

Chapter 18
Initiation
The Awakening

In Celtic culture, the transition from childhood to adulthood was not an automatic event, marked only by chronological age. It was a gradual process that involved learning, challenges, trials, and finally, a ritual of initiation. This ritual symbolized the community's recognition that the young person had acquired the skills, knowledge, and maturity necessary to assume their responsibilities as an adult member of the tribe.

The preparation for initiation began long before the ritual itself, often from childhood, permeating every moment of the young Celt's life. It was not just a technical or physical learning, but a complete journey of maturation, where each teaching had its right time to be assimilated.

From an early age, boys and girls were instructed by their parents, relatives, and other members of the tribe, absorbing essential knowledge for survival and the harmonious functioning of the community.

Boys were initiated into the arts of hunting and fishing, learning to track animals, set traps, and handle weapons such as spears and bows. Skill in combat was also essential, and so they trained hard with swords and shields, developing agility, strength, and strategy. In addition, they became apprentices to the tribe's artisans, working with metals to forge weapons and tools, erecting wooden and stone structures, and caring for the herds that ensured everyone's livelihood. Respect for nature was a fundamental principle; knowing the cycle of the seasons, interpreting the signs of the earth, and understanding the properties of plants were part of daily learning.

But not only practice defined their education— they also received instruction on the laws and customs of the tribe, immersing themselves in the history of their ancestors so that they would know where they came from and where they should lead future generations. The druids played a crucial role in this aspect, guiding them in the spiritual mysteries and understanding of the universe.

Girls, in turn, received an equally complex and vital education. From an early age, they learned to manage the home, ensuring that the family had shelter and sustenance. Cooking was not just a necessity, but a sacred knowledge that involved the alchemy of ingredients and respect for food. They spun and wove, mastering techniques that allowed them to produce resistant and beautiful garments, often adorned with protective symbols. The art of sewing and embroidery was also linked to their connection with the cycles of life, as was the cultivation of the land, where they learned to identify medicinal herbs and use them to cure ailments.

Their learning, however, was not limited to the domestic space. They also knew the history, laws, and customs of the tribe, and some, depending on the tradition, received teachings from the druidesses, being instructed in the divinatory arts, the secrets of healing, and reverence for the divinities. Feminine wisdom was an essential pillar of Celtic culture, and honoring the cycles of nature and their own existence was part of the path to maturity.

But knowledge alone was not enough to determine readiness for adulthood. It was necessary to prove it in practice. Before initiation, young people went through a series of challenges and tests that put their strength, intelligence, courage, and character to the test. Each tribe had its own traditions and specific tests, but some tests were common among the Celts.

Physical tests required resistance and survival skills. A young man might be challenged to hunt a wild animal alone, not only to demonstrate skill in handling weapons, but also to prove that he was capable of supporting himself. Other challenges involved spending days isolated in the forest, climbing mountains, swimming in icy waters, or enduring adverse conditions without any help. It was a way to ensure that, when they needed it, they would be ready to face the difficulties of adult life.

Skill in an art or craft was also fundamental, and so came the tests of skill. A blacksmith's apprentice could be challenged to forge a resistant blade; a young poet, to compose verses that captured the essence of his lineage; a healer, to identify and prepare an effective potion. Mastery in a craft not only showed competence, but also defined the role that the individual would assume within the tribe.

In addition, intellectual challenges were equally important. Young people should demonstrate knowledge about the history of the tribe, answer questions about laws and customs, identify constellations, and interpret omens. It was essential that they understand not only the physical world, but also the spiritual one.

Courage was one of the most valued attributes among the Celts, and therefore there were specific tests to test it. Some rites required the young person to face their fears directly, such as crossing a dense forest at night, hunting dangerous prey, or defending a member of the tribe in a simulated battle. In some traditions, they were subjected to experiences of isolation or deprivation, where they needed to demonstrate resilience and strength of spirit.

The spiritual journey was, finally, one of the most profound moments of initiation. Guided by druids or druidesses, young people could be led to altered states of consciousness through fasting, meditation, or the use of sacred herbs. Some went through shamanic journeys in search of a vision that revealed their mission in life. Others needed to demonstrate their connection with the gods and ancestors, understanding the mysteries of existence and accepting the cycle of life and death.

When the moment of the initiation ritual finally arrived, it was carried out with great solemnity, marking the young person's transition to adulthood. The preparation for the ritual was essential—for days, the young person underwent purifications, took ritual baths, and was smoked with sacred herbs. Fasting and meditation were part of the process, allowing him to reflect on his journey and prepare for the new path that was opening up.

In some traditions, the young person spent a period isolated in nature before the ritual, symbolizing the death of his childhood. This time alone or accompanied by a mentor served to reinforce his connection with the spirits and test his ability to survive on his own. When he returned, he wore special clothes that represented his new condition. Some tribes wore white clothes, symbolizing a pure rebirth, while others incorporated the colors and symbols of the lineage to which they belonged.

The most important moment of the ritual was the presentation of the young person to the community. Everyone gathered to recognize him as an adult, and he took a solemn oath, committing himself to his tribe, his gods, and the values that would guide his life. Then, he received symbols of his new phase—men could earn a weapon, while others received an amulet of power, a new name, or even a sacred tattoo. Finally, the druids and elders of the tribe blessed the young man, ensuring him protection and strength for his new journey.

The ceremony ended with a great celebration. The people gathered to celebrate, with plenty of food, drink, music, and dance. Games and challenges were also part of the festivities, symbolizing the energy and vitality of the new adult member of the community.

Even though times have changed and we no longer live in Celtic tribes, the essence of these rituals can be redeemed to mark the transitions of modern life. Creating our own rites of passage can bring a profound meaning to important moments, such as graduations, weddings, career changes, or challenges overcome. We can establish a period of reflection and preparation, face challenges that take us out of our comfort zone, choose symbols that represent our transformation, and share these moments with mentors and loved ones. The important thing is that the ritual has a true meaning for us, allowing us to honor our journey and embrace the new phase with awareness and courage. After all, initiation is always an awakening to what we truly are and to the role we choose to play in the world.

The important thing is to create a ritual that is meaningful to us, that helps us to mark the transition, to celebrate our achievements, and to prepare ourselves for the challenges and opportunities of the new phase of life. Initiation, in any era, is a moment of awakening, of recognizing our own power and assuming our responsibilities as individuals and as members of the community.

Chapter 19
Sacred Unions

In Celtic culture, marriage, or the Sacred Union, was much more than a legal contract or a simple social formality. It was a profound ritual, laden with symbolism, that celebrated the union of two souls, the connection with the land, fertility, and the continuation of life. It was a community event that involved not only the couple but also their families and the entire tribe.

In Celtic culture, the Sacred Union transcended any legal or social formality, being a true rite of passage that symbolized the connection between two souls, the balance between opposing forces, and the continuity of life. For the Celts, marriage was not just a commitment between individuals but a link between families, clans, and even between the human and divine worlds. This vision reflected the belief that harmony in the marital union reverberated throughout the community, bringing fertility to the land, prosperity to livestock, and abundance to harvests.

The Celts understood life as an interconnected cycle, where each aspect influenced the other. Thus, matrimony was more than a simple commitment; it was a sacred alliance, governed by values such as love, respect, and mutual trust. The connection between the couple should be balanced and fair, without submission, but with cooperation and mutual support. The symbolism of the union also reflected the fusion of masculine and feminine principles, of heaven and earth, of the sun and moon, forming a perfect unity within the natural order.

Within this context, the Celts had various forms of marriage, each adapted to the needs and circumstances of the time. Marriage by contract, called Lánamnas, was the most common and consisted of a formalized agreement between families, determining issues such as dowry, responsibilities, and possible conditions for separation. This type of union ensured stability and security for both those involved and the community. Experimental marriage, known as Teltown Marriage, allowed the couple to live together for a year and a day before deciding whether they wished to remain together. This practice valued mutual knowledge and compatibility, reducing the possibility of unhappy unions. There was also marriage by abduction, a less frequent tradition, but still present in some regions, where the groom "kidnapped" the bride – with her consent – and took her to his home, consolidating the union in a symbolic and romantic way. In contrast, political marriages were arranged to strengthen alliances between tribes and influential families, ensuring stability and power.

The Celtic wedding ceremony was enveloped in rituals deeply rooted in the spirituality of the people. Before the celebration, the couple underwent a period of preparation that included fasting, ritual baths, and meditation, as well as receiving advice from the elders. The choice of location for the ritual was also significant, and could take place in sacred groves, stone circles, springs, or hills, places impregnated with mystical energy.

On the day of the ceremony, the attire played an essential role. The couple wore garments in light tones or that represented their clans, and the bride often wore a crown of flowers or a veil, while the groom wore a brooch or bracelet. As a community event, the entire tribe participated, witnessing the union and sharing the blessings granted by the gods.

The ritual was conducted by a druid or a druidess, spiritual figures of great respect, who invoked the gods to bless the couple. Then, the bride and groom exchanged vows of love and fidelity, and could opt for traditional formulas or personalized words that reflected their deepest feelings. One of the most striking moments was the handfasting, the binding of hands with a ribbon or cord, symbolizing the connection between the two. The color of the fabric had specific meanings: red for passion, green for fertility, white for purity, or the colors of the clans, reinforcing family ties.

In addition, the couple exchanged symbolic gifts, which could vary between jewelry, weapons, tools, or significant objects. Another tradition involved the blessing of fire and water: jumping over a bonfire represented purification, renewal, and passion, while being bathed with sacred water symbolized fertility and fluidity. To conclude the ceremony, offerings were made to the gods and ancestors, and a great banquet was held, full of music, dance, and celebration, strengthening the bonds between those present. The wedding cake, often sweetened with honey and fruit, was part of the festivities, representing the sweetness and abundance of the new phase of life.

In modern times, many couples are inspired by Celtic rites to create personalized ceremonies full of meaning. Elements such as handfasting, the exchange of unique vows, the invocation of the gods – for those who follow this belief – and outdoor celebration rescue the ancestral connection with nature. The choice of location can reflect the essence of the couple, whether it be a grove, a beach, a mountain, or a special garden. Clothing and accessories can incorporate Celtic symbols and natural elements, reinforcing the individuality and spirituality of the couple.

More than a simple contract, the Sacred Union is a testament to the love and connection between two souls, honoring ancestral traditions and perpetuating the essence of a deep and lasting bond, blessed by nature and the gods.

The important thing is to create a ritual that celebrates the love, commitment, and union of the couple, that honors their roots and their beliefs, and that is an unforgettable moment for them and for all those present. The Sacred Union, more than a contract, is the celebration of a deep and lasting bond, blessed by nature and the gods.

Chapter 20
Healing Rites

In Celtic culture, health was viewed holistically, as a state of equilibrium between the body, mind, spirit, and environment. Illness, in turn, was understood as an imbalance, a disruption of this harmony. Celtic healing rites, therefore, sought to restore this equilibrium, using a variety of methods that combined the practical knowledge of the medicinal properties of plants, the connection with the energies of nature, the invocation of the gods, and the power of intention and visualization.

The Celts understood health in a broad way, considering it as a state of balance between body, mind, spirit, and environment. Thus, illness was not seen merely as a physical problem, but rather as a disruption of this harmony, which could have emotional, mental, or even spiritual origins. When someone fell ill, Celtic healers – whether they were druids, wise women, or other experts in the healing arts – sought not only to alleviate the symptoms, but also to understand the underlying cause of the problem.

Thus, a simple malaise could have diverse origins. A persistent headache, for example, could be caused by muscle tension related to poor posture or excessive exertion, but it could also be a reflection of worries, anxieties, and emotional stress. Furthermore, in a spiritual view, it could be associated with energy blockages or a detachment from nature and the vital forces that governed existence. Healers, therefore, analyzed all aspects of the patient's life: their diet, their daily habits, the quality of their relationships, their repressed emotions, and even their connection with the invisible world, seeking to restore the lost balance and harmony.

The healing methods used were diverse and often combined to meet the specific needs of each case. Among them, herbalism occupied a central role. The Celts possessed vast knowledge about the properties of medicinal plants, using roots, flowers, bark, and leaves to prepare teas, infusions, tinctures, ointments, and healing baths. Each herb was associated not only with specific therapeutic properties, but also with divinities and energies that reinforced its effect. Sage, for example, was used for purification and protection, while rosemary aided memory and mental clarity. Lavender was appreciated for its relaxing and calming effect, chamomile helped with digestion and reduced inflammation, calendula accelerated the healing of wounds, and mint was widely used for digestive problems and to invigorate the body and mind.

Hydrotherapy was also a common practice. Water, considered sacred, was used for both purification and treatment of diseases. Thermal springs, rivers, and lakes were chosen according to their properties, and it was believed that certain places had healing waters, associated with beneficial divinities. Ritual baths, compresses, and immersions were used to relieve pain, remove energetic impurities, and restore the body's vitality.

Another fundamental element was chromotherapy, which used colors to balance the body's energy centers. Green was associated with healing and regeneration, blue with tranquility and strengthening communication, and yellow with stimulating creativity and joy. Crystal therapy also played an important role, as crystals were seen as conductors of specific energies. Clear quartz, for example, was used for purification and energetic amplification, amethyst for spiritual protection, and rose quartz for issues related to love and emotional healing.

Therapeutic touch was another resource employed by healers. With their hands, they channeled healing energies, relieving pain, relaxing muscles, and promoting general well-being. These practices could be compared to modern forms of energy healing, such as Reiki, or even therapeutic massages that aid circulation and the body's energy flow.

Although less common, there were also records of surgical practices among the Celts. One of the most intriguing procedures was trepanation – the drilling of the skull – which may have been used to relieve extreme headaches, treat convulsions, or even release energies considered negative. Although rudimentary by today's standards, this technique demonstrates a surprising anatomical knowledge for the time.

In addition to physical practices, Celtic healing also involved magic and enchantments. Healers recited prayers, used sacred symbols like the Ogham, and performed rituals to invoke the help of the gods, ancestors, and natural forces. Each word spoken carried an intention, and it was believed that the vibration generated by the enchantments had the power to transform reality.

Another essential aspect was counseling and emotional support. Often, physical problems were manifestations of unresolved internal conflicts. Thus, healers listened to their patients attentively, offering guidance so that they could understand their pain and find paths to inner healing.

Sleep and dreams were also valued in this process. It was believed that, during rest, the soul could travel to other realms, receive messages from the gods, and find answers to life's challenges. Dreams were interpreted as signs and, in some cases, used as diagnostic tools by healers.

Music and dance, in turn, were incorporated into healing rituals to elevate energy and facilitate altered states of consciousness. Drums, flutes, and harps were used to create rhythms that favored connection with the divine and promoted emotional release.

When a healing ritual was performed, it followed a specific structure. First, there was the preparation of the healer and the patient, which involved purifying baths, fumigation with herbs, and, in some cases, fasting. Next, the sacred space was delimited and purified, usually in forests, springs, or circles of stones. The invocation of spiritual forces occurred through prayers, chants, and the use of instruments. The diagnosis of the disease was made with careful observation, reading of the aura and, in some cases, divination with Ogham or runes. Treatment included the use of herbs, crystals, hydrotherapy, healing touches, enchantments, or even surgeries, depending on the case. After the application of the cure, offerings were left in gratitude to the spiritual forces that had helped in the process. The patient also received guidance on changes in their life, and subsequent monitoring was done to ensure that the cure was consolidated.

In modern times, although we cannot replicate these rites exactly as they were practiced by the Celts, we can be inspired by this ancestral wisdom to adopt healthier and more integrative habits. The conscious use of medicinal herbs, connection with nature, relaxation and meditation practices, a balanced diet, care with emotions and spiritual development are ways to apply this knowledge in a way adapted to modern reality. Complementary therapies, such as aromatherapy, crystal therapy and Reiki, can also be explored, always with the guidance of qualified professionals.

The most important thing is to understand that healing is a holistic and profound process, which involves not only the body, but also the mind and the spirit. By seeking balance and reconnection with nature and the divine, we can restore our health more completely and significantly.

It is important to remember that the ancient Celtic healing rites were performed by people with deep knowledge and experience, and that we should not try to replicate them without proper guidance and preparation.

However, we can be inspired by their ancestral wisdom to seek a more balanced, healthy and connected life with nature and the divine. Healing, ultimately, is a process of self-discovery, transformation and integration of all aspects of our being.

Chapter 21
Celtic Divination

Divination was an important practice in Celtic culture, used to obtain guidance, predict the future, make decisions, understand the signs of nature, and connect with the spiritual world. The Celts believed that the veil between worlds was thin and that it was possible to access information and wisdom from the Otherworld through different methods.

The Celtic view of divination went beyond a simple prediction of the future; it was a means of seeing possibilities, understanding trends, and grasping influences that could shape events. The Celts did not see destiny as something unchangeable, but rather as a constantly transforming flow, subject to individual choices and actions. Thus, divination was seen not as an infallible oracle, but as a guide, a way to access ancestral and spiritual wisdom to make decisions more aligned with one's own path in life.

For them, this practice functioned as a bridge between worlds, allowing communication not only with the gods, but also with ancestors, nature spirits, and even one's own unconscious. Through it, it was possible to obtain advice, insights, and directions to live in a way more connected to one's personal destiny. Thus, Celtic divination was not just a mystical art, but a tool for everyday life, employed with respect and wisdom.

Celtic divination methods were diverse, varying according to the need of the moment and the preference of the practitioner. One of the most respected and widely used systems was the Ogham, the sacred alphabet of the trees. Each of its letters was associated with a specific tree, carrying deep symbolism and magical properties. There were several ways to use the Ogham for divination. In the method of throwing sticks, pieces of wood with the letters carved on them were thrown onto a surface, and the position in which they fell determined their interpretation. Another approach was the choice of sticks, where a set of them was placed inside a bag and, without looking, the consultant withdrew one or more, interpreting the letters drawn according to their meaning. In addition, some versions of the Ogham were adapted to a format similar to that of Tarot cards, allowing the symbols to be drawn on cards and used for oracle readings.

Another essential means of obtaining messages from the Otherworld was the observation of signs from nature. The Celts were masters in the art of interpreting the movements of the environment around them, believing that nature was constantly communicating with those who knew how to listen. The flight of birds was one of the most analyzed signs: the direction in which they flew, their height in the sky, the species of the bird, and even the animal's behavior were considered significant omens. Similarly, the behavior of other animals could indicate answers to important questions.

Unexpected encounters with certain creatures, their movements, or even the sounds they made were seen as messages from the spirits. The clouds were also carefully observed, as their shapes could reveal symbols and figures with hidden meanings. Natural elements, such as the sound of wind and water, carried whispers from the Otherworld, serving as guides for those who knew how to listen to them with an open heart. Extraordinary natural phenomena, such as eclipses, comets, and storms, were interpreted as divine signs, announcing changes, challenges, or blessings that were to come.

Dreams had a central role in Celtic divination, being considered windows to other realms. It was believed that, while sleeping, the soul could travel to places beyond physical reality, meeting with gods, ancestors, or spirits who transmitted valuable messages to it. For this reason, the interpretation of dreams was a revered practice, and those who had the ability to decipher them were sought to guide entire communities. The druids, in particular, were experts in this art, helping individuals understand nocturnal visions and extract wisdom for their lives.

Scrying, or vidency, was another common technique among the Celts. It consisted of staring at a reflective surface – such as the water in a bowl, an obsidian mirror, a crystal, or even the flame of a candle – in order to obtain images and intuitive revelations. The practitioner concentrated deeply, allowing their mind to transcend the physical plane and access hidden information. This method required a high degree of sensitivity and training, being usually practiced by druids and experienced seers.

Intuition, in turn, was seen as a precious gift and cultivated with dedication. For the Celts, the ability to feel and understand the subtle energies around was a fundamental component of divination. Developing intuition required daily practices, such as meditation, contemplation of nature, fasting, and even rituals of contact with the spiritual realms. The diviner trained their spirit to capture messages that were not always visible to common eyes, becoming a channel between the human world and the forces of the beyond.

In addition to these methods, there were also less common, but equally powerful practices. Some traditions mentioned the reading of the entrails of sacrificed animals – a custom more frequent among the Romans, but which could also be found in certain Celtic contexts. Another technique involved observing the flames of a bonfire and interpreting their movements, colors, and crackles. Finally, there were those who read patterns formed randomly, such as the throwing of stones or bones, seeking hidden meanings in the arrangement of the elements.

The Celtic diviner was a figure of extreme importance within society. He was not only a prophet of the future, but a counselor, a spiritual guide, and often a healer. His function was to help people understand their dilemmas, make crucial decisions, and reconnect with their ancestors. Many of these diviners were druids, bards, or wise women, holders of deep knowledge about the mysteries of the universe. They played a fundamental role in maintaining the balance between worlds, ensuring that the signs were understood and respected.

In modern times, we can still be inspired by the ancestral methods of Celtic divination to strengthen our intuition and spiritual connection. The study of Ogham continues to be a powerful practice, allowing its messages to guide those who seek wisdom. The observation of signs of nature can be incorporated into our daily lives, from noticing the flight of a bird to noticing patterns in the wind or water. Paying attention to dreams and seeking to interpret them helps us access messages from the subconscious and more subtle planes. Scrying, using black mirrors or bowls of water, can be an excellent tool for those who wish to develop their intuitive perception.

In addition, we can adapt these practices to modernity, using tools such as Tarot, runes, or other oracles. However, it is essential to maintain a respectful and conscious approach, remembering that divination is not a mere pastime, but a journey of self-knowledge and growth. More than seeking ready answers, we must use it as an instrument to better understand our path, make wiser decisions, and live with more meaning and purpose.

Finally, it is fundamental to remember that divination should not be seen as an absolute truth. Interpretations can vary, and discernment is necessary to apply them in our lives. We must always trust our own intuition and free will, using divination as support, but never as a substitute for our ability to think, feel, and act. If used with responsibility and wisdom, this ancestral art can be a powerful ally in the search for self-knowledge and connection with the mysteries of the universe.

It is important to remember that divination is not an exact science and that interpretations can vary. We must use divination with responsibility, discernment and common sense, always trusting our own intuition and our free will. Divination can be a powerful tool for self-knowledge and for making decisions, but it should not replace our own ability to think, feel and act.

Chapter 22
Transition and Death

In Celtic culture, death was not seen as an end, but as a transition, a passage to the Otherworld, a realm of eternal youth, beauty, and abundance. The Celts believed in the immortality of the soul and in reincarnation, and therefore, death was viewed with a mixture of sadness for the loss of a loved one, but also of hope and celebration for their journey to a new cycle.

The Celts had a unique view of death, seeing it not as a definitive end, but as a passage to a new phase of existence. For them, the soul was immortal and continued its journey in the Otherworld, a realm filled with magic, eternal youth and fullness. The concept of reincarnation was deeply rooted in their beliefs, being seen not as a cycle of suffering, but as a continuous opportunity for learning and evolution. The Otherworld, known by various names, such as Annwn or Sidhe, was described as an enchanted place, where gods, ancestors and fairy beings lived. This supernatural domain could be accessed in sacred places such as hills, caves, lakes or forests. Thus, death was interpreted as a transition and not an abrupt end, representing a necessary transformation within the great cycle of existence.

Respect and connection with ancestors were fundamental elements for the Celts. They believed that the dead not only remained spiritually present, but also exerted influence over the living, offering protection and wisdom. Communication with those who had departed was possible through rituals, dreams and divinatory practices. Furthermore, death was inserted into the Wheel of Life, a concept that represented the natural flow of existence, in which birth, growth and death continuously succeeded one another, guaranteeing balance and renewal.

Celtic funeral rituals were rich in symbolism and varied according to the time, region and social status of the deceased. The first step was the preparation of the body, which included its cleaning and clothing with special garments, such as a white shroud. Often, the body was adorned with jewelry, amulets and symbols painted on the skin, representing protection and safe passage to the Otherworld. Then came the wake, a moment of great importance, where family and friends gathered to pay homage. This period could last from a few hours to weeks, during which ceremonies were held that included chants, accounts of the deceased's achievements and symbolic offerings.

The final destination of the body could follow two main paths: cremation or burial. In the Bronze Age and early Iron Age, cremation was the predominant practice. The body was placed on a funeral pyre and burned along with personal belongings and offerings, a symbolic act that facilitated their journey to the Otherworld. The ashes were then stored in urns and buried in sacred places. Over time, burial became more common, and the body was buried in simple graves, stone tombs or elaborate burial chambers. Alongside the deceased, significant objects were deposited, such as weapons, tools, food and even animals, believing that these items would accompany them on their new journey.

Mourning was not just a period of pain, but also a moment of celebration of life. The funeral banquet, held after the burial, brought the community together to share food, drink, music and dance, strengthening bonds and ensuring that the memory of the deceased remained alive. This event symbolized the acceptance of death as part of the natural cycle. In addition, mourning practices involved dietary restrictions, wearing dark clothes and performing daily remembrance rituals.

Reverence to ancestors was not limited to funerals. Festivals such as Samhain, celebrated on October 31st, marked times when the veil between the worlds became thinner, allowing communication between the living and the dead. During this period, it was common to leave offerings for the spirits and light candles in honor of those who had departed, reaffirming the Celtic belief that death was just a new phase of the journey.

Nowadays, it is possible to adapt Celtic teachings to create more meaningful and personalized farewell ceremonies. Elements such as holding a wake at home or in a special place help to make the farewell more intimate and connected with ancestral traditions. In addition, ecological forms of burial, such as natural burials without a coffin or cremations with the planting of trees, rescue the Celtic vision of harmony with nature.

Personalized rituals can be incorporated to mark the passage of a loved one, including the reading of poems, music, dances and even the burning of incense. The ceremony can take place outdoors, in woods, beaches or mountains, reinforcing the connection with the earth and with the cycle of life. Elements that honor ancestors, such as the display of photos and personal objects, also help to strengthen the bond with those who came before us.

Mourning, in its most genuine expression, should be respected and allowed without judgment. Creating spaces where pain can be shared and understood is essential for emotional healing. Just as the Celts celebrated life in their funeral rituals, we can rescue this vision and transform the farewell into a moment of honor and gratitude for the existence of the deceased. Mutual support between family and friends becomes fundamental in this process, helping to soften the pain of loss and reaffirm the continuity of life.

More than a goodbye, death can be seen as a moment of transformation and connection with the sacred. Creating rituals that resonate with our history and beliefs allows us to honor those who have departed and, at the same time, strengthen our own journey.

The important thing is to create a ritual that is meaningful for us and our family, that honors the memory of the deceased, that celebrates their life and that helps us to deal with the pain of loss and move forward. Death, as a natural part of life, can be a moment of deep reflection, transformation and connection with the sacred.

Chapter 23
The Awakening of the Celtic Soul

Celtic spirituality, with its profound connection to nature, its reverence for ancestors, its celebration of the cycles of life, and its belief in magic and the Otherworld, offers a rich and inspiring path to the awakening of the soul. More than a set of rituals and practices, Celtic spirituality is a way of life, a way of seeing and interacting with the world that can help us find a deeper meaning for our existence and live more authentically, fully, and connectedly.

Awakening the Celtic soul is not a question of ancestry or place of birth, but an internal call that resonates deeply in those who feel the need to reconnect with ancestral wisdom, with nature, and with the magic present in all things. This awakening manifests itself in various ways and can involve a personal journey of self-knowledge and spirituality.

First, there is the reconnection with nature, one of the fundamental pillars of Celtic spirituality. This implies not only appreciating the beauty of the natural world, but recognizing the sacredness of the earth, plants, animals, and elements. The relationship with nature is established through careful observation, respect for natural cycles, and the search for a harmonious coexistence with living beings. Practices such as meditative walks in forests, river or sea baths with purifying intentions, and even the cultivation of medicinal plants can be ways to strengthen this bond. Furthermore, understanding the cycles of the seasons and experiencing each one of them consciously is a way to align oneself with the energies of the earth.

Honoring ancestors is another essential aspect of this awakening. For the Celts, the ancestors continued to exert influence in the world of the living, offering protection and guidance. Creating an altar dedicated to ancestry, lighting candles in their memory, or simply remembering their stories and teachings are ways of paying this tribute. One can establish a moment of the day or month to reflect on their lives, thank their contributions, and ask for their wisdom for the challenges of the present.

Celebrating the cycles of life is also part of this journey. The Celts saw time in a cyclical way, and their celebrations were marked by the changes of the seasons, such as the festivals of the Wheel of the Year. These moments were not just external rituals, but opportunities for introspection and renewal. Participating in these celebrations, whether in groups or individually, can strengthen the sense of belonging and spiritual connection. Simple rituals, such as lighting a candle at Samhain to honor the dead or planting seeds at Beltane to symbolize new beginnings, bring this spirituality into everyday life.

The awakening of intuition is also a central point. For the Celts, the world was permeated by signs and omens, and developing the ability to interpret them was a valuable skill. Exercises such as the practice of silence, attentive listening to nature, observation of dreams, and meditation with Celtic symbols help to improve this sensitivity. The Ogham, the alphabet of the trees, can be used as a tool to access symbolic messages and insights, providing a deeper connection with the language of nature.

Creativity, in turn, was considered a manifestation of the divine. The Celtic bards channeled their inspiration through poetry, music, and art, believing that this expression was a link between the human and the sacred. Cultivating creativity can mean playing an instrument, writing, painting, dancing, or practicing any other activity that allows the free manifestation of the spirit. The important thing is that this expression comes from an authentic place, allowing the soul to speak through art.

Seeking balance between opposites is another valuable Celtic teaching. The balance between body, mind, and spirit, between light and shadow, between action and introspection is essential for a harmonious life. This can be achieved through practices such as meditation, conscious eating, and purification rituals that help to align energies. On the Celtic path, balance is also reflected in the respect for the duality of existence, accepting both moments of growth and periods of retreat as equally valuable parts of the journey.

Living with purpose is one of the natural developments of this awakening. The Celts believed that each being had a unique role in the great cycle of life and that recognizing and following this call brought fulfillment and plenitude. Discovering what one's personal mission is may require deep reflections, attempts, and adjustments along the way, but the search for authenticity is always rewarding. Following one's heart, acting according to one's own values, and contributing meaningfully to the world are ways of honoring this principle.

The connection with the divine occurs in an individualized and personal way. Some people find this connection through the veneration of Celtic gods and goddesses, others feel this presence through nature, the elements, or their spiritual guides. The important thing is that this relationship is genuine and comes from the heart. Creating one's own rituals, offering prayers, meditating, or simply spending time in sacred places are ways to cultivate this connection.

Living with authenticity is perhaps one of the most profound challenges and, at the same time, one of the greatest gifts of this path. Being true to oneself in a world that often imposes norms and expectations can be difficult, but it is also liberating. Honoring one's own truth, respecting one's own rhythms, and not conforming to patterns that do not resonate with the soul are ways of practicing this authenticity.

Finally, Celtic ethics guides the way of living and interacting with the world. Principles such as courage, generosity, respect, and honor are fundamental values that should be incorporated into everyday life. Being loyal to one's word, acting with integrity, and cultivating hospitality are practical ways of applying this ethic.

The Celtic teachings offer a vast and enriching path for those seeking this awakening. The Wheel of the Year, for example, allows a deep connection with the rhythms of nature, providing moments of reflection and renewal throughout the year. The study of Celtic symbols, such as the triskle and the triquetra, helps in the understanding of deep spiritual concepts. The practice of rituals strengthens the connection with the divine and allows the manifestation of intentions. Natural magic, with the use of herbs, crystals, and the elements, expands the perception of the subtle energy around us.

Another valuable aspect of this journey is Celtic mythology. Its stories full of gods, heroes, and magical beings carry timeless lessons that can inspire and guide. The study of the Druidic tradition, with its focus on wisdom, healing, and service to the community, offers a model of structured spiritual growth. The path of the bard, the ovate, and the druid represents the stages of this search for knowledge and personal improvement.

However, this awakening is not without challenges. It may require facing limiting beliefs, overcoming fears, and the willingness to leave one's comfort zone. Integrating these teachings into a modern world often focused on materialism can be an arduous task. However, the rewards are immeasurable: greater connection with nature, personal growth, sharpened intuition, blossoming creativity, emotional balance, well-being, and a deep sense of belonging and purpose.

The awakening of the Celtic soul is an invitation to live in a more conscious, connected, and authentic way. It is not a goal to be achieved, but a continuous path of learning and transformation. It is the rediscovery of an ancient wisdom that still beats in the hearts of those who feel the call of the earth, the ancestors, and the magic that permeates everything around them.

The awakening of the Celtic soul is a continuous journey, a path of learning, growth, and transformation. It is an invitation to live more consciously, connectedly, and fully, honoring ancestral wisdom and the magic that exists within us and around us.

Chapter 24
Gratitude Rituals

Gratitude is one of the most important virtues in Celtic spirituality, a key to happiness, abundance, and connection with the divine. The Celts, with their deep connection to nature and the cycles of life, understood the power of gratitude and expressed it in their rituals, prayers, songs, and daily life.

The Celts understood gratitude not just as a passing feeling, but as a fundamental principle of existence, a daily practice capable of transforming life into a harmonious flow of reciprocity and blessings. For them, giving thanks was an act of aligning with the forces of nature, a recognition that all that is received must be honored so that the cycle of abundance continues. Gratitude was seen as an energy that opened doors to prosperity, strengthened the connection with the divine, helped in overcoming challenges, promoted well-being, and sustained the foundation of reciprocity.

The practice of gratitude was incorporated in various ways into Celtic spirituality, from simple gestures in everyday life to elaborate rituals that celebrated the gift of life. One of the simplest and most powerful rituals was the Morning Prayer of Thanksgiving. Upon waking, even before getting out of bed, it was customary to set aside a few minutes to give thanks for life, health, the new day that was beginning, loved ones, and all the blessings received. Gratitude could be expressed through a spontaneous prayer, words murmured in thought or recited aloud, or even through traditional prayers. An example of a Celtic prayer used in these moments was:

"Great Spirit, I thank you for this new day, For the light of the sun that warms me, For the air that I breathe, For the earth that sustains me, For the water that purifies me, For the fire that transforms me, For the life that beats within me. May I honor your gifts with wisdom and love."

In addition to prayer, the Celts had the habit of offering gifts to nature as a form of recognition for its generosity. This ritual of Offerings to Nature consisted of leaving symbolic offerings in sacred places, such as groves, rivers, mountains, or ancestral stones. Flowers, fruits, grains, seeds, honey, and milk were some of the most common offerings, always given with respect and sincere intention. Before making the offering, it was essential to ask permission from nature and express gratitude for what had already been granted. The gesture reinforced the idea that everything in life is an exchange and that receiving also requires giving back.

Another important custom was the creation of an Altar of Gratitude. This sacred space, set up inside the home, served as a daily reminder of the blessings received and the need for recognition. The altar could contain photos of loved ones, symbols of achievements, memories of happy moments, elements of nature, crystals, candles, and incense. Spending a few minutes daily in front of this altar, meditating on the gifts of life and expressing gratitude, helped to strengthen the energy of gratitude and maintain awareness of what really matters.

Recording reasons for gratitude was a valuable practice for the Celts, and a Gratitude Journal fulfilled this function. The idea was simple: to write daily about the small and large blessings of the day, from a smile received to a significant achievement. This habit allowed the mind to be trained to perceive and value daily gifts, cultivating a more positive attitude and recognizing abundance in all areas of life.

Expressing gratitude in community was also common. The Circle of Gratitude was a ritual where friends, family members, or members of the tribe gathered to share reasons for gratitude. Each person spoke of something for which they were grateful, creating an atmosphere of celebration and mutual recognition. Songs, collective prayers, and stories were shared, strengthening the bonds between participants and reinforcing the energy of gratitude as a collective force.

The Celts also kept alive the practice of Thanksgiving to Ancestors. They recognized that all they had—their knowledge, their culture, their roots—came from those who came before. Honoring ancestors was a way of thanking them for this legacy. To do this, they created altars with photos or symbols of their ancestors, lit candles, made offerings, and even visited the resting places of their relatives to meditate and connect with their energies. This reverence helped to strengthen the feeling of belonging and continuity.

In sacred festivals, gratitude was a central theme. During the Gratitude Rituals in the Celtic Festivals, each celebration of the ancestral calendar included specific moments to give thanks. At the Samhain festival, the Celts expressed their gratitude to their ancestors. In Yule, they thanked for the return of light. In Imbolc, they honored purification and the inspiration received. Ostara marked gratitude for the rebirth of life, while Beltane was a time to thank for love and fertility. Litha celebrated the strength of the sun and abundance, Lughnasadh the harvest, and Mabon the balance of life. Each of these sacred dates was an opportunity to recognize and celebrate the blessings of the natural cycle.

But gratitude was not expressed only in formal rituals—it needed to be lived. The practice of Gratitude in Action involved transforming gratitude into concrete gestures, being kind and generous to the people around you, helping those in need, taking care of the environment, and using talents and abilities to improve the world. Small acts of kindness, respect, and generosity were seen as ways of giving back to the universe all that was received.

To deepen this experience, many Celts practiced Gratitude Meditation. This simple exercise consisted of setting aside a few minutes of the day to enter a state of relaxation, close your eyes, and bring to mind everything for which you were grateful. Visualizing the people, situations, and events that brought happiness helped to reinforce a positive state of mind, allowing gratitude to expand and permeate every aspect of existence.

Gratitude did not need a specific moment to be expressed. The Spontaneous Celebration was a reminder that, throughout the day, whenever something good happened or whenever the beauty of life was perceived, it was important to stop for a moment and give thanks. Celebrating the small joys, the simple moments, and the gift of being alive was a constant practice, a reminder that life is a gift and that every moment can be honored.

Gratitude, for the Celts, was not a mere formality, but a way of life. By cultivating it consciously and intentionally, they created a continuous cycle of blessings, where abundance flowed freely and the connection with the divine was strengthened. This practice, even today, can transform lives, bringing more joy, peace, and purpose to each journey. May gratitude always be a light to guide our steps and illuminate our path.

Gratitude is a powerful practice that can transform our lives. By cultivating gratitude in our daily lives, we open our hearts to abundance, strengthen our connection with the divine, and live with more joy, peace, and purpose. May gratitude be a constant in our journey, guiding our steps and illuminating our path.

Part IV
Deepening and Advanced Practice

Chapter 25
Advanced Celtic Magic

Celtic magic, at its core, is the art of working in harmony with the forces of nature and the Otherworld to manifest intentions, promote healing, and attain wisdom. Advanced Celtic magic involves delving deeper into these principles, exploring more complex techniques, establishing deeper connections with deities and spirits, and taking greater responsibility for one's own magical power.

Advanced Celtic magic is founded on essential principles that guide the practitioner on their magical journey, making them not just an executor of spells, but a true guardian of the forces of nature and the Otherworld. The first of these principles is a deep connection with nature. The advanced practitioner does not see nature as something external to be exploited, but as an extension of themselves. They carefully observe the seasons, the lunar cycles, the flow of the tides, and the patterns of the winds. Walking through a forest, smelling the scent of damp earth after rain, perceiving the dance of leaves in the wind - all of this becomes a constant dialogue with natural spirits. The energy of trees, the song of rivers, and even the silence of mountains carry messages that the practitioner learns to decipher. They thus become a conscious channel of this living energy, learning to direct it for healing, protection, and spiritual growth.

The relationship with Celtic deities is another fundamental pillar. Instead of merely invoking the gods and goddesses in moments of need, the advanced practitioner cultivates a constant connection with them. This is done through sincere prayers, symbolic offerings, and moments of contemplation before a dedicated altar. This altar may contain images, statues, or symbols of the gods, candles representing their presence, crystals to amplify their energy, and offerings such as honey, milk, bread, or wine, depending on the deity honored. Additionally, the study of mythology is essential to understand the essence of each god and goddess, their domains, and how they interact with mortals. Through meditation, the practitioner learns to hear their guidance and feel their presence, strengthening a relationship that transcends simple request and response, becoming a true spiritual alliance.

The mastery of the elements - earth, air, fire, and water - is deepened as the practitioner evolves. They understand that each element has a personality, a unique vibration, and a specific function within magic. Earth represents stability, nourishment, and the materialization of desires; air symbolizes intellect, communication, and inspiration; fire carries the force of transformation, passion, and will; and water reflects emotions, intuition, and the fluidity of life. Working with the elements involves specific rituals, such as lighting candles to channel fire, using water sources in purification rituals, burning herbs to connect with air, or burying written requests in the earth to affirm intentions. Over time, the practitioner learns to balance these elements within themselves, harmonizing their internal energy with the primordial forces of the universe.

The manipulation of vital energy is a skill refined by the advanced practitioner. Known by various names - vital force, prana, chi, or odic energy - this energy permeates everything that exists and can be directed for various purposes. One of the most effective methods for working with this energy is conscious breathing. Inhaling deeply, visualizing the energy entering through the top of the head and descending through the body, and exhaling releasing blockages or stagnant energies, helps to strengthen the energy flow. Furthermore, techniques such as laying on of hands for healing, energetically drawn circles of protection, and projection of intentions through visualization become part of the practitioner's arsenal. The key to effective manipulation lies in controlling one's own mind, in focus and clear intention.

The use of symbols and magical tools gains greater depth in advanced practice. The Ogham, the ancient Celtic alphabet, is not just an oracle, but a system of power. Each of its feda (letters) carries a specific vibration and can be engraved on talismans, carved on sacred staffs, or used in written enchantments. Celtic knots, with their intertwined and infinite designs, are more than art: they are expressions of the continuity of life, the interconnectedness of all things, and the power to bind or release energies. Tools such as the athame (ceremonial dagger), wand, chalice, and pentacle are used with precise intention, each representing an aspect of the cosmos and serving to channel power more effectively. The practitioner learns that true power is not in the objects themselves, but in the energy and intention they project through them.

Ethics and responsibility become more rigorous as the practitioner advances on their path. They understand that magic is not a game and that every action has a consequence. The Triple Law, which states that all energy sent out into the world returns multiplied by three, becomes an essential guideline. Furthermore, the principle of not harming anyone governs every spell, avoiding any form of manipulation or interference with the will of others. The pursuit of knowledge is incessant, for magic is not something static, but a path of continuous learning. The practitioner reads, experiments, observes the results, and refines their practices with discipline and respect.

Advanced techniques of Celtic magic involve a wide spectrum of possibilities. The Ogham can be used not only for divination but also for the creation of amulets engraved with specific symbols to attract protection, prosperity, or healing. The magic of Celtic knots allows the practitioner to tie or release situations, binding unwanted energies or undoing blockages by untying the knots. Magic with the elements teaches how to invoke and evoke elemental beings, such as sylphs, salamanders, ondines, and gnomes, asking for their help in specific rituals. The influence of weather can be worked with extreme respect, attuning to natural rhythms to attract rain, dispel storms, or invoke fog for protection.

The use of crystals deepens, including the creation of energy grids to amplify intentions and the preparation of magical elixirs. Work with herbs expands to include ritual baths and powerful smudges. Dream magic becomes a tool for guidance and healing, and the practitioner advances in the development of astral projection. Thought-forms are created and directed with precision, shaping reality in a subtle but powerful way.

The connection with the Moon intensifies, and rituals are adjusted for each lunar phase, harnessing its energy for specific purposes, such as new beginnings in the New Moon, growth in the Waxing Moon, manifestation in the Full Moon, and banishment in the Waning Moon. The honor to ancestors strengthens, and the practitioner establishes deep spiritual ties with those who came before, receiving their wisdom and protection.

Advanced Celtic magic is, above all, a path of personal and spiritual transformation. It demands commitment, respect, and a genuine desire for growth. By treading this path with ethics and wisdom, the practitioner awakens their true power, becoming a link between the visible and invisible worlds, a guardian of ancient magic, and an agent of balance and harmony in the universe.

Advanced Celtic magic is a path of profound transformation that demands commitment, discipline, and respect. By treading this path with wisdom and ethics, the practitioner can awaken their inner power, connect with the forces of nature and the Otherworld, and contribute to a more magical and harmonious world.

Chapter 26
Shamanic Journeys

Shamanic journeys are an ancestral practice found in various cultures around the world, including the Celtic tradition. They are journeys of consciousness, induced through techniques such as the beating of the drum, the rattle, dance, chanting, meditation, or the use of power plants - in some traditions - which allow the practitioner to access other states of reality, connect with their spiritual guides, power animals, and ancestors, and gain insights, healing, and wisdom.

Celtic Shamanism, although not named as such in its time, involved deeply spiritual practices and connection with the invisible worlds. Despite the Siberian origin of the term "shamanism," altered states of consciousness for healing and knowledge were common among the Celts, with the druids being their main conductors. They were not only priests but also healers, counselors, poets, and guardians of ancestral knowledge. Masters of magic, divination, and astronomy, the druids understood the natural cycles and communicated with the spirits of the earth, the gods, and the ancestors. Although there are no direct written records of their practices - since their tradition was essentially oral - archaeological and mythological evidence suggests that they used methods similar to those of other shamanic cultures around the world.

The Celtic shamanic journey was an incursion of consciousness through varied techniques, allowing the exploration of other realms of existence. Each experience was unique but usually followed a basic structure. The first step was preparation, which began with defining the intention of the journey. Before starting, the practitioner needed to establish what they were seeking - whether it was healing, guidance, knowledge, or spiritual connection. This purpose would guide the entire experience. Creating a sacred space was also essential. This environment should be protected and free from distractions, and could be either in nature or a reserved place within the home, such as an altar. To purify this space and the practitioner themselves, fumigation rituals with herbs such as sage, cedar, or rosemary were common, as was the use of salt water, sounds like bells and drums, or even guided visualizations. In addition, invoking protection was a fundamental step. The practitioner could ask for help from their spiritual guides, gods, ancestors, or beings of light, visualizing a protective shield of energy around them.

The induction of the altered state of consciousness was one of the central aspects of the journey and could be achieved in various ways. The constant rhythm of the drum - between 4 to 7 beats per second - was one of the most effective ways to enter a trance, allowing the mind to detach from everyday reality. The rattle was also used, both to induce the altered state and to purify and energize the environment. Ecstatic dance, with repetitive and rhythmic movements, led the practitioner to a condition of ecstasy, where it was possible to move between worlds. Chanting played a similar role, whether through mantras, songs of power, or spontaneous vocalizations. Guided meditation, with specific images and instructions, was another way to facilitate the journey, as were deep and rhythmic breathing techniques, such as holotropic breathing. Some traditions made use of power plants, such as ayahuasca, peyote, or psilocybin mushrooms, to intensify the experience. However, this method was considered extremely delicate and dangerous, and should only be conducted under the supervision of an experienced shaman, within an appropriate ritualistic context.

Once in an altered state, the practitioner began their spiritual journey. With their eyes closed, they visualized an entrance to the Otherworld - which could manifest as a cave, a hole in a tree, a waterfall, or any portal that resonated with their intuition. Upon crossing this threshold, they entered the spiritual realm, where they would encounter their guides, power animals, ancestors, or divinities. During this journey, they could receive messages, teachings, and even spiritual healings. The Otherworld was not a single fixed space but a mutable environment, composed of different realms and dimensions that could be explored according to the need and guidance received.

Upon completing the journey, the practitioner should make a conscious return. The first step was to respectfully say goodbye to the spiritual guides and thank them for the experience. Then, they visualized themselves returning along the same path they had come, bringing with them the knowledge acquired. Upon reopening their eyes, grounding was essential to reintegrate into the physical world. Feeling their feet on the ground, breathing deeply, and drinking water helped to restore energetic balance and avoid feelings of disorientation.

Recording the experience was a crucial step for the assimilation of the knowledge received. Writing in a journal allowed the practitioner to organize their perceptions, recording visions, messages, and feelings experienced. Drawing or painting images associated with the journey was also a powerful form of integration. If desired, they could share their experience with a mentor, trusted friend, or shamanic practice group.

In Celtic cosmology, the universe was divided into three interconnected worlds. The Upper World, equivalent to Heaven, was the domain of gods, goddesses, and celestial beings, being a place of learning, inspiration, and spiritual transcendence. The Middle World represented the Earth, where humans, animals, plants, and the spirits of nature lived. It was the realm of manifestation, sensory experience, and everyday life. The Lower World, or Underworld, did not have a negative connotation, but rather a deep meaning of power, transformation, and rebirth. It was the place of ancestors, power animals, and chthonic forces, where fears were faced and a more instinctive and primordial wisdom was accessed. Depending on the practitioner's intention, the journey could take them to any of these worlds.

Power animals were fundamental spiritual allies in the Celtic shamanic journey. Each animal possessed specific characteristics, symbolism, and gifts that aided the practitioner in their journey. The deer represented nobility, grace, and leadership, as well as symbolizing the connection with wild nature. The crow was the messenger of the Otherworld, bringing mystery, magic, and transformation. The wolf carried the attributes of loyalty, intuition, and freedom, being a powerful guide for those seeking their wild spirit. The bear represented strength, courage, and healing, assisting in introspection and inner strengthening. The salmon symbolized wisdom, overcoming challenges, and returning to origins. The eagle was a symbol of broad vision, clarity, and connection with the divine. The swan carried the energy of beauty, grace, and transformation, while the serpent represented rebirth, healing, and deep ancestral knowledge.

Being a powerful practice, the shamanic journey required responsibility and respect. Always seeking guidance from an experienced practitioner, beginners could prepare themselves adequately for their first spiritual incursions. Ensuring a safe and protected environment was essential for the experience to be conducted without external interference. In addition, avoiding substances such as alcohol and heavy meals before the journey helped to keep the mind and body receptive. Trusting intuition and accepting the messages received without resistance were attitudes that facilitated connection with the spiritual world. Like any skill, the shamanic journey required practice and patience to become deeper and more revealing over time. After each experience, integrating the learning into everyday life allowed the spiritual teachings to become a source of growth and personal transformation.

Following the path of the shamanic journey was, therefore, a choice of self-discovery and healing, an invitation to access ancestral wisdom and strengthen the connection with the sacred. By treading this path with respect and dedication, the practitioner could not only know their own inner power but also live in a more balanced and meaningful way.

The shamanic journey is a path of self-discovery, healing, and connection with the sacred. By exploring this ancestral practice, you can awaken your inner power, access the wisdom of your spiritual guides, and live a fuller and more meaningful life.

Chapter 27
The Druidic Tradition

The Druidic tradition is one of the pillars of Celtic spirituality, a path of knowledge, wisdom, magic, healing, and connection with nature and the divine. Druids were the priests, judges, counselors, doctors, teachers, poets, and guardians of the ancestral wisdom of the ancient Celts.

Druids were much more than simple priests within Celtic society. They were considered the intellectual and spiritual elite, guardians of an ancestral knowledge passed down from generation to generation. Their responsibilities went far beyond the performance of religious rituals; they were advisors to kings, judges in charge of justice, doctors who mastered healing through herbs and the energies of nature, as well as poets and bards who preserved the history and culture of the Celtic people through orality. The importance of druids in society was such that their training required decades of learning, involving astronomy, philosophy, magic, and a deep understanding of natural and spiritual laws.

Within their functions, the druids stood out as priests and priestesses, responsible for performing religious ceremonies, seasonal festivals, and offering rituals to the gods, always in harmony with the cycles of nature. In addition, they acted as judges and legislators, interpreting tribal laws and resolving disputes between members of the community. Their role as counselors was essential, as they guided political leaders and warriors in strategic decision-making, based both on tradition and on the careful observation of the signs of nature. In the field of medicine, they were respected healers, connoisseurs of the therapeutic properties of plants and practitioners of healing methods that combined science, spirituality and magic. Their wisdom also extended to education, being responsible for teaching young apprentices who would later assume their places as holders of Druidic knowledge.

The bards, in turn, were the guardians of the collective memory, using music and poetry to preserve and transmit the history and mythology of the Celtic people. Druids also played the role of seers and diviners, resorting to Ogham - the alphabet of trees - and the interpretation of the signs of nature to guide the future and advise leaders. Above all, they were guardians of nature, living in total respect and harmony with the natural elements and recognizing the sacredness of every living being.

Druidic philosophy was based on essential principles that guided their conduct and understanding of the world. They believed in the sacredness of nature, considering it a manifestation of the divine. Every tree, river, mountain, animal, and star was revered as part of a sacred whole. Furthermore, they recognized the interconnectedness of all things, understanding that everything in the universe was intertwined and that every action reverberated in the balance of the world. The immortality of the soul was a certainty for the druids, who saw death not as an end, but as a passage to the Other World, from where the spirit could return through reincarnation. They incessantly sought the balance between opposites - light and darkness, masculine and feminine, life and death - because they believed that harmony was the key to health and happiness. Above all, they valued knowledge and wisdom, dedicating their lives to the study and transmission of learning. They practiced Druidic ethics, based on values such as generosity, courage, honor, hospitality and respect for truth, in addition to following the Triple Law, according to which all energy emitted returns multiplied.

The Druidic organization was structured hierarchically, divided into three main classes. Bards were the poets, musicians, and storytellers, responsible for preserving Celtic culture and history through oral tradition. The ovates, or vates, were diviners and healers, specialists in the interpretation of natural signs and communication with the spiritual world. The druids themselves were the philosophers, judges, and masters, responsible for the spiritual and intellectual guidance of the community. There were also druidesses, women who played similar roles to male druids, with emphasis on the areas of healing, divination, and connection with nature.

Druidic training was an arduous and lengthy process, which could last up to twenty years.

Apprentices received teachings transmitted orally by their masters, covering a wide range of knowledge. They studied astronomy and cosmology to understand natural cycles and the movement of the stars, as well as mathematics and geometry, essential for the construction of monuments and ritual calculations. Botany and herbology were fundamental to the mastery of the medicinal and magical properties of plants, while zoology deepened the understanding of the behavior and symbolism of animals. Druidic medicine combined the use of herbs, incantations, and even rudimentary surgical techniques in certain cases. Knowledge of laws and justice was equally essential, allowing druids to act as arbiters and legislators within society.

Celtic history and mythology were taught in detail, ensuring that apprentices became guardians of the memory of their people. Poetry and music played a central role, as the spoken word possessed a magical power within the Druidic tradition. Divination methods, such as reading the Ogham and interpreting natural omens, were also part of the curriculum, as were magical practices and rituals. Druidic philosophy and theology taught about the nature of the divine, reincarnation, and the fundamental principles of universal balance.

With the Roman conquest of Gaul and Britain and the subsequent Christianization of the British Isles, the Druidic tradition began to decline. The druids were persecuted, their sacred groves destroyed, and their rituals banned. However, Druidic wisdom did not disappear completely; it survived in legends, folklore, and even within Christianity, influencing popular culture over the centuries.

From the 18th century onwards, Druidic revivalism emerged as a movement that seeks to rescue and reinterpret this ancient tradition for modern times. Today, various Druidic orders and groups exist around the world, each with their own approaches and practices. Contemporary Druidry continues to honor nature, ancestors and Celtic spirituality, adapting to the needs and challenges of today's society.

If you wish to connect with the Druidic tradition, there are several ways to do so. The first step is to study and research, reading about Druidic history, mythology and philosophy. Spending time in nature and developing a bond of respect with the natural cycles is essential. Celebrating the festivals of the Wheel of the Year, such as Samhain, Beltane and Imbolc, helps to align with the seasonal rhythms. The study of Ogham can serve as an oracle and meditation tool. Regular meditation practice aids in the development of intuition and connection with the divine. In addition, expressing yourself creatively through art, music or writing can be a powerful way to channel the Druidic essence.

If you want a deeper experience, seeking a Druidic group or order can be a valuable option, as long as you research the group's suitability before getting involved. Finally, living according to Druidic ethical principles - based on honor, justice, courage, generosity and respect for life - is the most authentic way to incorporate this ancient wisdom into everyday life.

The Druidic tradition is a path of wisdom, connection with nature and the divine, and service to the community. By drawing inspiration from the ancestral wisdom of the druids, we can find a deeper meaning for our lives and contribute to a more balanced, just and harmonious world.

Chapter 28
The Path of the Bard

In Celtic tradition, the bard held a prominent place in society, being much more than a mere musician or poet. He was the guardian of the collective memory, the transmitter of the history, mythology, and values of his people. Through the sung word, poetry, and music, the bard inspired, educated, entertained, and connected people with the past, present, and future.

The bard occupied an essential role in Celtic society, and his responsibilities went far beyond music and poetry. He was the guardian of the people's memory, the transmitter of ancestral stories, and a link between the past and the present. His song, his word, and his music carried deep teachings, keeping alive the cultural identity of the community.

Within this function, he performed several fundamental tasks. As a preserver of history and tradition, he was responsible for retaining and orally transmitting the narratives of his people, from family genealogies to the heroic deeds of gods and warriors, without forgetting the laws and customs of the tribe. This knowledge was not recorded in writing, which made his memory one of the greatest treasures of Celtic society.

In addition, the bard also acted as an educator, passing on moral values, ancestral knowledge, and the skills necessary for young people to fully integrate into adult life. His role as a counselor was also of great importance, because, armed with his wisdom and a broad vision of history and human nature, he guided leaders and members of the community in decisive moments.

Inspiring was another of his most sublime functions. With his songs and poems, he inflamed the courage of warriors before battles, exalted the victories won, and lamented the defeats, giving meaning and depth to collective emotions. His gift for art also made him an animator of festivities and celebrations, ensuring that music, poetry, and stories created an environment of joy and union among all.

Furthermore, the bard was a chronicler of the most significant events of his time. Poetic compositions recorded heroic deeds, battles, matrimonial unions between noble families, and other events of relevance to the collectivity. His influence did not stop there, as he also played the role of mediator in disputes, resorting to his eloquence and intelligence to seek peaceful resolutions to conflicts.

Finally, the bard possessed a critical function within society. Through sharp satires, he could expose weaknesses and injustices, revealing political or social problems in an artistic and insightful way, without the need for force or violence.

The training of a bard was a long and demanding journey, which could take years until the apprentice mastered all the necessary skills. Those chosen to follow this path were usually young people endowed with a natural talent for words and music. Guided by experienced masters, they received intense oral training, absorbing a vast repertoire of stories, laws, and teachings.

Among the fundamental aspects of this learning, memorization was one of the most challenging. Without the aid of writing, the bard needed to retain in his mind an immense amount of poems, songs, stories, and genealogies. This ability to remember and recite long texts with precision was an essential characteristic of his craft.

Poetic composition was also part of his formation. He learned the techniques of meter, rhyme, alliteration, and other stylistic structures, acquiring the ability to create verses on demand for the most diverse occasions. No less important was the mastery of music, since the bard should play instruments such as harp, lyre, flute, or drum, incorporating melodies that amplified the emotional impact of his poetry.

To perform his role with excellence, he needed a deep knowledge of the history and mythology of his people. This included the study of the genealogies of influential families, the myths of gods and heroes, the laws and tribal customs. Oratory was another essential pillar of training, allowing the bard to develop a clear, expressive, and persuasive speech.

In addition to his technical skills, the bard also needed to refine his observation of the world around him. He should be able to capture nuances of nature and human interactions, using these perceptions in his compositions. All of this was guided by a strong ethical code, which valued truth, justice, courage, generosity, hospitality, and respect for the gods and ancestors.

The musical instruments that accompanied the bard were varied and essential for his presentations. The harp was the noblest among them, emitting a soft and deep sound, capable of touching the soul of the listeners and transporting them to elevated states of emotion. The lyre, smaller and simpler, was used for lighter and joyful music, while the flute, made of wood, bone, or metal, evoked sweet and melancholic melodies, in addition to imitating sounds of nature. The drum marked the rhythm of dances, war songs, and rites of ecstasy, while the crwth, a stringed instrument played with a bow, produced unique and engaging tones.

Although the ancient bardic tradition has dissipated over time, its spirit remains alive in contemporary times. The path of the bard can still be followed by those who feel the calling of art, music, and the word as forms of connection, inspiration, and transformation.

To follow this path today, a first step is to study Celtic culture, delving into its history, mythology, and spirituality through books, articles, and research. Music, being a vital element of the bard's path, can be explored through learning an instrument, such as harp, flute, guitar, or drum, allowing musicality to be incorporated into the personal journey.

Poetic writing is also a powerful way to express feelings, ideas, and experiences, being an essential exercise for those who wish to awaken their bardic side. Similarly, the art of storytelling can be cultivated, whether through the narration of traditional Celtic legends, the preservation of family memories, or the creation of original stories.

Singing is another essential practice for those who wish to revive the bardic tradition. Singing traditional, folk, or own compositions can strengthen the connection with this ancestry. In addition, seeking a study group or a bardic circle, whether in person or online, can provide an enriching exchange with other enthusiasts of this path.

Celebrating Celtic festivals and participating in the rituals of the Wheel of the Year can also deepen the connection with this path, allowing for a closer experience of the cycles of nature and the divine archetypes that govern each season. Developing oratory, practicing public speaking and using the word with eloquence and consciousness, is another essential aspect to honor this tradition.

The word has power, and the bard understood this deeply. Therefore, using it with wisdom and responsibility is fundamental. It should serve to inspire, educate, heal, unite, and build, never to hurt, manipulate, or destroy. Thus, by following the path of the bard in the present day, it is possible to become a guardian of memory, preserving and transmitting the history, culture, and values that connect us to our roots and to the future.

This path is, above all, an invitation to beauty, creativity, and depth. By following this journey, creative potential is awakened, the inner voice is strengthened, and the wisdom of the ancestors is honored, contributing to a more inspired, harmonious, and meaningful world.

Chapter 29
The Warrior's Path

In Celtic society, warriors held a place of honor and respect. They were the defenders of the tribe, the protectors of the land and the people, those responsible for maintaining order and security. But the path of the Celtic warrior was not just about physical strength and combat skills. It was also a path of inner development, of discipline, courage, honor, and connection with the divine.

Celtic warriors were much more than mere soldiers. Their bravery and ferocity in combat made them feared by their enemies and admired by their allies, but their importance within the tribe went beyond war. They played multiple roles, fundamental to the survival and balance of the community. As defenders of the tribe, their primary responsibility was to ensure security against external attacks, invasions, and any threat that could endanger the lives of their people. However, their mission was not limited to protection against human enemies; they were also guardians of the land, responsible for preserving natural resources, ensuring that the forest, rivers, and animals were respected and used sustainably.

Furthermore, their presence was essential to maintain order and justice within the tribe. When disputes arose between members of the community, warriors often acted as mediators or executors of decisions made by leaders and druids. They were also role models of courage and honor for all, serving as an inspiration to young people and reminding everyone of the importance of loyalty, strength, and dignity. In some traditions, warriors underwent initiation rituals that not only prepared them for battle but also connected them to the spiritual world. The belief that they were connected to the gods of war and ancestral spirits was part of their training, providing them with a strength that went beyond the physical.

Hunting was another essential activity in their routine. It not only provided meat to feed the tribe but was also practical training for combat, requiring stealth, precision, and endurance. Warriors also had the sacred duty to protect the most vulnerable in the community, including children, the elderly, and the sick. For them, a true warrior was not one who merely wielded a sword but one who used his strength to ensure the well-being of his people.

From childhood, the young man who wished to follow this path was subjected to rigorous training. Their combat skills were developed with different types of weapons, such as sword, spear, bow, and shield, in addition to mastering horsemanship and, in some regions, the use of the chariot. Physical training was intense, aimed at developing strength, endurance, and agility through daily exercises, running, jumping, and even practices such as swimming. However, preparation was not limited to the body; the mind and spirit were also molded. Strategy and tactics were taught so that the warrior knew when to attack, when to retreat, and how to surprise his opponents. Survival in nature was another essential skill: learning to find food and water, build shelters, make fire, and orient themselves ensured that a warrior never depended exclusively on civilization to survive.

Self-control and mental discipline were equally crucial. The warrior should learn to master fear and pain, remaining firm even in the face of death. Courage did not mean the absence of fear, but the ability to act despite it. And this courage should be guided by a code of honor that determined the behavior of warriors inside and outside the battlefield. This code was not written but passed down orally, rooting deep values such as loyalty to the tribe and companions, honesty in all actions, justice in the protection of the weak and in the punishment of offenders, generosity towards the needy, and hospitality towards strangers. Respect was equally fundamental, encompassing defeated enemies, the dead, the gods, and nature itself.

Honor was the basis of everything. Keeping one's word, fulfilling promises, and acting with dignity were principles that guided their lives. The worst fate for a warrior was not death, but dishonor, for losing honor meant losing everything that made him a true warrior.

Although today we no longer live in a tribal and warlike society, the teachings of the Celtic warrior's path remain relevant. We can still develop courage, not necessarily to face physical enemies, but to face the challenges of life, overcome fears, and fight for what we believe in. Inner strength, whether physical, mental, or emotional, allows us to resist adversity and continue moving forward. Living with integrity means acting with honesty, loyalty, and justice, maintaining our principles even when it puts us at a disadvantage.

We can also apply the principle of protecting the weakest, whether by helping those in need, fighting injustices, or being a voice for those who have none. Honoring our commitments is a way of demonstrating responsibility and character, fulfilling promises and taking responsibility for the consequences of our choices. Seeking self-knowledge allows us to understand our strengths and weaknesses, our fears and desires, helping us to live more authentically and in line with our essence.

The connection with nature, something fundamental to the Celts, can be brought back into our modern routine. Spending time outdoors, respecting natural cycles, and learning from the wisdom of the earth help us maintain an inner balance. Developing discipline, setting goals, and persisting even in the face of difficulties are practices that bring us closer to the warrior spirit, preparing us to face any obstacle with determination.

Finally, finding a purpose greater than ourselves is one of the greatest lessons of the warrior's path. It is not just about battles or individual achievements, but about contributing to something greater, whether helping our community, protecting nature, or serving an ideal that transcends our personal ambitions.

The warrior's path, today, is a path of self-discovery, overcoming challenges, and service. It is an invitation to awaken our potential, live with courage, and leave our positive mark on the world.

Chapter 30
The Healing of the Earth

In Celtic spirituality, the Earth is seen as a living, sacred, and powerful being, the very manifestation of the Mother Goddess. The Celts believed that the health and well-being of the Earth were intrinsically linked to the health and well-being of its people. Therefore, caring for the Earth, honoring it, and healing it was a sacred responsibility.

For the Celts, the Earth was not just a piece of rock and inert soil, but a living, pulsating, and conscious being, endowed with its own energy and spirit. They recognized it as the Great Mother, the origin of all life, the primordial source that nourished, protected, and sustained all creatures. Its fertile womb was the cradle of forests, rivers, and mountains, and its breath of life permeated every corner of the natural world. Thus, honoring it was not only an act of gratitude but a vital necessity for the harmony of the universe.

The personification of the Earth as a goddess was something natural within Celtic spirituality. In different regions and traditions, she assumed diverse names and aspects, reflecting the unique characteristics of each culture. In Ireland, she was venerated as Danu, the primordial mother goddess, considered the ancestor of all the gods and goddesses of the Tuatha Dé Danann pantheon. Her presence was the very manifestation of the flow of creation, magic, and abundance. In Wales, her equivalent was Don, revered as the great matriarch of the divine lineage. Anu, also from the Irish tradition, represented the fertile earth, prosperity, and abundance, being especially associated with the region of Munster, where twin hills known as "Breasts of Anu" symbolized her nurturing presence. Tailtiu, in turn, was remembered as the goddess of agriculture and harvest, guardian of cultivated soil and crops. Among the Welsh, Modron embodied the essence of sacred motherhood, connecting the earthly world to the Otherworld, ensuring the cyclical renewal of life.

These goddesses reflected the vital energy of the Earth and its immense capacity to generate, sustain, and transform life. They personified its ancestral wisdom and its power of healing, which manifested itself both in the fertility of the soil and in the renewal of the waters and the strength of the winds. However, just as human beings could get sick and weaken, the Earth was also subject to wounds and imbalances caused by mistreatment and disrespect for its natural balance.

When the Celts observed abrupt changes in nature, they interpreted them as signs that the Earth was suffering. Natural disasters, such as violent storms, prolonged droughts, devastating floods, earthquakes, and volcanic eruptions, were seen as cries from the Great Mother, expressing her pain and asking for healing. The emergence of pests and diseases that affected animals, plants, and humans was considered a symptom that the sacred cycle of life was broken. The infertility of the soil, the impoverishment of crops, and the scarcity of food indicated that the vitality of the Earth was diminished, requiring rituals of restoration. Furthermore, it was believed that even conflicts and wars reflected the illness of the natural world, since the disharmony among men was a mirror of the imbalance of the Earth itself.

To restore the health of the planet, the Celts performed various healing rituals, seeking to re-equilibrate the energies and honor the sacredness of the Earth. Offerings were a common and essential practice in these rituals. Food, drinks, flowers, herbs, crystals, and symbolic objects were left in sacred places such as forests, rivers, mountains, and stone circles, as a form of thanksgiving and reconnection. These symbolic acts demonstrated respect and reverence, strengthening the bond between the people and the Earth.

Prayers and incantations were also recited with fervor, invoking the help of the gods, ancestors, and spirits of nature. These chants and sacred words had the power to vibrate in the spiritual fabric of the world, transmitting intentions of healing and repentance for the damage caused. Music and dance were used as powerful tools to raise energy and restore harmony. With rhythmic steps and circular movements, the Celts channeled their connection with the Earth, generating a current of vital force capable of revitalizing natural spaces.

The cleaning of rivers, forests, and other sacred sites was an act of respect and responsibility. By removing pollution and garbage, the Celts recognized their role as guardians of the Earth, understanding that healing required concrete actions. The planting of trees was another deeply significant gesture. Each seedling cultivated represented not only a gift to nature but a renewal of the commitment to care for the planet. Trees were seen as wise beings, bridges between worlds, capable of purifying the air, providing shelter and sustenance for countless creatures.

Creating sacred spaces was also a way to contribute to the restoration of the Earth. Gardens, orchards, and consecrated groves were cultivated with devotion, serving as sanctuaries for wildlife and for the spiritual growth of those who maintained them. The Celts believed in the importance of working directly with the four elements – earth, air, fire, and water – to balance energies and promote regeneration. Specific rituals were performed to harmonize these primordial forces, ensuring that each element was in tune with the others.

The Celtic shamans played a crucial role in this healing process. Through spiritual journeys, they connected with the invisible realms, seeking to understand the deeper causes of the Earth's suffering and receiving guidance for its restoration. Their rites could involve deep meditations, contact with spirit guides, and the channeling of healing energies to the affected places.

In our days, this connection with the Earth and the need to heal it are more urgent than ever. The environmental crisis we face demands a profound change in our relationship with the planet. To be inspired by the ancestral wisdom of the Celts can be a valuable way to cultivate a more sustainable and respectful lifestyle with the environment. Small individual and collective actions can make a big difference: reducing rampant consumption, recycling, reusing materials, and opting for ecological products are practical ways to minimize our negative impact.

Spending more time in nature, understanding its cycles, and learning from its lessons strengthens our connection with the natural world. The planting of trees, the creation of gardens, and the protection of green spaces are gestures that perpetuate the Celtic tradition of honoring the Earth. Furthermore, engaging in environmental movements, participating in clean-up efforts, and defending the preservation of biodiversity are ways to put respect for the Great Mother into practice.

Conscious consumption also plays a fundamental role in this healing. Choosing organic and local foods, supporting small producers, and avoiding products that excessively exploit natural resources are attitudes that benefit both the Earth and human communities. Educating new generations about the importance of environmental preservation is essential to ensure a more balanced future.

Finally, the Earth healing rituals can be adapted to our modern reality. Symbolic offerings, guided meditations, chants, dances, and visualizations are powerful ways to channel positive energy to the planet. Every action, however small it may seem, contributes to restoring harmony between human beings and the Earth.

By rescuing the ancient Celtic wisdom and applying it in our daily lives, we become an active part of this healing process, ensuring a more sustainable and sacred future for all forms of life.

The healing of the Earth is an urgent and necessary task, which demands the participation of all of us. By adopting a more conscious, respectful, and loving posture in relation to the planet, we can contribute to the construction of a more sustainable, just, and harmonious future for all forms of life. May the ancestral wisdom of the Celts inspire us and guide us on this journey.

Chapter 31
Living Celtic Spirituality

Celtic spirituality is not just a set of beliefs and practices to be followed at specific times, but a way of life, a way of being in the world, which permeates all our actions, thoughts and relationships. Living Celtic spirituality means integrating its principles and values into our daily lives, seeking to live more consciously, connected and authentically.

The journey to integrate Celtic spirituality into our daily lives begins with a fundamental step: daily connection with nature. Nature is not merely a setting for Celtic life, but its very essence, the foundation on which everything is built. It is vital, therefore, to make a conscious effort to connect with it every day. Imagine starting your day with a walk in a park, allowing your senses to awaken to the symphony of natural life. Observe the majesty of the trees, each with its silent history engraved in the rings of its trunk, the vibrant and delicate colors of the flowers, the aerial dance of the birds and the inspiring vastness of the sky, which reminds us of our connection with the cosmos. Don't just look; feel. Let the warmth of the sun caress your skin, the cool breeze caress your face, and the firmness of the earth nourish your bare feet. These tactile sensations are powerful ways to anchor ourselves in the present and recognize our belonging to the natural world. If possible, create a small garden, even a miniature garden in pots or planters. The act of cultivating, of accompanying the growth of a plant, of feeling the earth between your fingers, is a meditation in itself. Bring nature into your home with plants, which purify the air and gladden the spirit. Observe the phases of the moon, its cyclical dance in the night sky, and the cycles of the seasons, the eternal turning of life, death and rebirth. And above all, practice gratitude. Thank nature for its unparalleled beauty, for its generous abundance that sustains us, and for its ancestral wisdom that guides us. This daily thankfulness establishes a deep and personal bond with the source of Celtic spirituality.

Furthermore, Celtic spirituality invites us to honor the cycles of life. Life is not a straight line, but a perpetual cycle of birth, growth, decline, death and rebirth. Recognizing and honoring these cycles within ourselves is fundamental. Celebrate with joy the moments of expansion, growth, achievements, but accept with serenity and learning the moments of sadness, recollection, challenges. These less luminous moments are not failures, but integral parts of the cycle, opportunities for introspection and renewal. Learn from your mistakes and challenges, using them as stepping stones for personal and spiritual growth. Like the leaves that fall in autumn to make way for a new cycle in spring, learn to let go of what no longer serves you, limiting beliefs, negative behavior patterns, toxic relationships, thus opening space for the new, for the flourishing of new possibilities. Celebrate the rites of passage with meaningful rituals that mark these important transitions in life. Birthdays, graduations, weddings, births, and even deaths, are key moments that can be enriched with ceremonies that honor the passage, the change, the cycle of life. These rituals confer depth and meaning to these stages, connecting us with the natural rhythm of existence.

Gratitude emerges as a powerful practice, a golden thread that weaves Celtic spirituality. It is a key that opens doors to the abundance of life, to recognize the gifts that are constantly offered to us. Start and end your day with a moment dedicated to gratitude. Give thanks for the good things that exist in your life, whether they are big or small, material or spiritual, visible or invisible. Give thanks for health, home, family, friends, food, a stranger's smile, the beauty of the starry sky. Keep a gratitude journal, a sacred space where you can record daily the things for which you feel grateful. This simple but profound act helps to train your eyes for the positive, for the beautiful, even in the most challenging days. And don't forget to express your gratitude to the people who are part of your life, a gesture of recognition that strengthens bonds and nurtures relationships.

In addition to gratitude, Celtic spirituality encourages us to develop our intuition, the voice of the soul, the inner wisdom that resides in each of us and that guides us on the path of life. In a world dominated by logic and reason, we often forget to listen to that silent but persistent voice that whispers deep truths to us. Set aside time to silence the mind, quiet the whirlwind of thoughts and emotions, and open space for intuition to manifest. Meditation, the practice of mindfulness, time spent in nature, writing in a diary, creative activities, are valuable tools to access this inner space of wisdom. Trust your instincts, those visceral sensations that often indicate the right path, even if it seems to go against logic or the opinion of others. Intuition is an internal compass that guides us to our most authentic truth.

The connection with the past, with our roots, is another pillar of Celtic spirituality, which manifests itself in the practice of honoring ancestors. Ancestors are not just figures of the past, but sources of wisdom, strength and inspiration that continue to influence our lives. Research your family tree, explore the history of your family, discover the stories and legacies of your ancestors. Create an altar dedicated to your ancestors, a sacred space where you can place photographs, personal objects that belonged to them, and symbolic offerings, such as flowers, candles, or incense. Talk to your ancestors in thought or aloud, ask for their guidance and protection, feel their presence and support. Honor the memory of your ancestors by living a worthy and meaningful life, carrying their legacy with pride and respect.

The expression of creativity is seen in Celtic spirituality as a vital force, a manifestation of our divine essence, the spark of creation that resides in each of us. Find ways to express your creativity in your daily life, releasing that creative energy that longs to manifest itself. Write poems, stories, songs, paint pictures, draw mandalas, sing ancestral melodies, dance to the rhythm of nature, cook tasty dishes, make crafts with your hands, play a musical instrument, cultivate a flower garden. Don't worry about perfection, about the judgment of others, just let your creativity flow freely, like a river that runs to the sea. Creativity is a form of prayer, a way of connecting with the divine that resides within us.

The backbone of Celtic spirituality is based on ethics and integrity. Honor, truth, justice, courage, generosity and hospitality are sacred values that should guide our actions and decisions in all areas of life. Strive to live according to these principles, cultivating honesty in your words and actions, fulfilling your promises, defending what you believe in, helping others and contributing to the well-being of the community. Integrity is the moral compass that guides us on the path of life, ensuring that our actions are aligned with our deepest values.

The thirst for knowledge and wisdom was a hallmark of the druids, the ancient Celtic priests. Remain an eternal learner throughout your life, seeking knowledge from various sources and areas. Read books that expand your mind and your spirit, take courses and workshops that inspire you, participate in enriching conversations with wise people, explore different areas of knowledge, from philosophy to science, from art to spirituality. But seek not only intellectual knowledge, bookish knowledge, but also practical knowledge, know-how, knowledge of the heart, emotional wisdom, and spiritual knowledge, the understanding of our connection with the divine.

In a society that constantly bombards us with appeals to consumption and material accumulation, Celtic spirituality offers a valuable counterpoint, inviting us to simplify our lives. Detach yourself from what is not essential, from the superfluous, from what only occupies physical and mental space. Reduce unnecessary consumption, free yourself from the clutter that oppresses the spirit, organize your time, prioritizing what is really important to you, to your happiness and well-being. Value the simple and true things in life, a sunset, the smile of a child, a conversation with a friend, the silence of nature. Simplicity is a form of freedom, a path to inner peace.

Hospitality was a sacred value for the Celts, a mark of their culture and spirituality. Open your home and your heart to others, receive your friends and family with generosity and joy, offer help and support to those in need, be welcoming to strangers and to those who are different from you. Hospitality creates bridges between people, strengthens community ties, and promotes understanding and empathy.

Care for health is seen in Celtic spirituality as an act of respect for the body, mind and spirit, a sacred temple that has been entrusted to us. Eat healthily, nourishing your body with fresh and natural foods, practice physical exercises that give you pleasure and vitality, sleep enough to restore energy, reduce stress, cultivate positive thoughts and emotions, seek therapies and practices that promote your integral well-being, such as meditation, yoga, or acupuncture. Health is a precious asset, a gift of life that we must cultivate and preserve.

Celebrating life in all its forms, in every moment, is a constant invitation from Celtic spirituality. Life is a sacred gift, a unique opportunity for learning, growth and experience. Dance, sing, laugh, play, love intensely, embrace with affection, smile with your heart. Enjoy every moment, live intensely, be grateful for being alive, for every breath, for every experience, for every encounter. The celebration of life is a way of honoring its sacredness.

Feeling like a guardian of the Earth, just as the ancient Celts did, is a responsibility that Celtic spirituality confers upon us. Recognize your intrinsic connection with the planet, with nature, with all living beings. Do your part, however small it may be, to care for the Earth, to preserve its beauty and its resources. Recycle trash, conserve water and energy, plant trees, reduce plastic consumption, and use sustainable transportation. Every small action counts, and together we can make a difference in protecting our common home, planet Earth.

Creating your own rituals is an act of autonomy and personalization of your Celtic spirituality. Use ancestral rituals and celebrations as inspiration, but adapt them to your life, your needs, your beliefs, and create your own rituals that resonate with your soul. The important thing is not to follow rigid rules or copy models from the past, but rather the intention you put into your rituals and the connection you establish with the sacred through them.

Finally, the search for a community is presented as an enriching option, although Celtic spirituality can be experienced individually. Finding a group of people with similar interests, who share the same spiritual quest, can be very valuable for exchanging experiences, learning from others, celebrating rituals together, and feeling part of something greater. Look for Celtic groups, orders, or circles in your region or online, but always with caution and discernment, seeking references and information about their seriousness and suitability. Sharing in community can strengthen your spiritual journey, but the choice to participate or not is always individual and respectable.

Living Celtic spirituality is, therefore, a continuous journey, a dynamic process of learning, growth, and transformation. It is not about following dogmas or inflexible rules, nor about trying to replicate the way of life of the ancient Celts, but rather about integrating their principles and values into your life in an authentic and meaningful way, awakening your own Celtic soul, connecting with ancestral wisdom, and living a fuller, more connected, and more magical life. It is a personal and unique path, an adventure of the spirit that unfolds with each step, with each cycle, with each celebration of life.

Living Celtic spirituality is a continuous process, a journey of learning, growth, and transformation. It is not about following rigid rules or becoming a copy of the ancient Celts, but rather about integrating their principles and values into your life in an authentic and meaningful way. In doing so, you can awaken your

Celtic soul, connect with ancestral wisdom, and live a fuller, more connected, and more magical life.

Chapter 32
The Celtic Legacy

Celtic culture, although it flourished millennia ago, left an enduring legacy that continues to influence the modern world in various ways. Whether in art, literature, music, spirituality, or values and customs, the Celtic heritage resonates in our society, inspiring us to seek a deeper connection with nature, with creativity, with the community, and with the sacred.

The Celtic legacy, woven over millennia, manifests itself in surprising and multifaceted ways in the contemporary world. Its influence permeates various areas of our culture, from the aesthetics of visual arts and design, through the richness of literature and music, to the spiritual quest and the values that shape our society. It is as if an invisible thread of connection links us to the ancient Celts, reminding us of an ancestral heritage that continues to live and vibrate.

In the realm of art and design, the Celtic mark is unmistakable. The intricate Celtic knots, with their intertwined lines that seem to have no beginning or end, the spirals that evoke movement and growth, the triskeles that symbolize the triplicity of life, and other enigmatic symbols continue to inspire artists, designers, and artisans around the world. These symbols, loaded with meaning and beauty, transcend time and cultural boundaries, finding expression in diverse forms of art and design. We can admire them in elaborate jewelry, adorning the body with its ancestral elegance, in clothes that incorporate Celtic motifs, conferring a touch of mysticism and tradition, in tattoos that eternalize the connection with the Celtic heritage on the skin, in decorative objects that embellish our spaces with their unique aesthetic, in illustrations that evoke fantastic and mythological worlds, in graphic design that visually communicates the Celtic essence, and even in architecture, where Celtic elements are integrated, conferring a distinctive and ancestral character. The persistence of these symbols over the centuries demonstrates their intrinsic power and their ability to resonate with the human soul, regardless of time or culture.

Literature, that mirror of the human soul, was deeply touched by Celtic mythology. The stories of powerful and complex gods, of courageous and fallible heroes, of magical creatures that inhabit enchanted realms, captivated the imagination of generations of writers and readers. Celtic mythology, with its symbolic and narrative richness, has become an inexhaustible source of inspiration for Western literature, leaving its indelible mark from the Arthurian legends, with their noble and mysterious knights, to contemporary fantasy works that transport us to imaginary worlds. Think of the Celtic influence in works like "The Lord of the Rings" by J.R.R. Tolkien, with its Middle-earth populated by elves, dwarves, and other fantastic creatures, or in "The Mists of Avalon" by Marion Zimmer Bradley, which revisits the Arthurian myth from the perspective of female figures. In addition to fantasy, authors such as W.B. Yeats, James Joyce, and other Irish writers, imbued with their cultural heritage, incorporated elements of the Celtic tradition into their works, exploring themes such as identity, nature, mysticism, and the history of Ireland, conferring them with a unique depth and authenticity. Celtic literature, with its magic and ancestral wisdom, continues to enchant and inspire, transporting us to worlds of dreams and reflection.

Music, the universal language of emotion, also received a valuable legacy from Celtic culture. Traditional Celtic music, with its characteristic instruments that evoke green landscapes and magical atmospheres, such as the harp, with its ethereal and celestial melodies, the flute, with its joyful and pastoral sounds, the violin, with its passionate expressiveness, and the bodhrán (drum), with its ancestral and pulsating rhythm, continues to enchant and inspire people in all corners of the world. The influence of Celtic music is vast and diverse, extending to various musical genres, such as folk, which rescued traditional melodies and rhythms, rock, which incorporated Celtic elements in arrangements and instrumentation, pop, which experimented with fusions with Celtic sonorities, and new age music, which found in Celtic music a source of inspiration for relaxing and meditative atmospheres. Contemporary artists continue to explore and reinterpret

Celtic music, keeping its flame alive and demonstrating its timelessness and universal appeal.

In the realm of spirituality, the Celtic tradition offers an alternative and enriching path for those seeking a deeper connection with the sacred. Celtic spirituality, with its emphasis on nature as a divine manifestation, on magic as a force present in the world, on reincarnation as a continuous cycle of life, and on the intrinsic connection with the divine that permeates all things, has attracted a growing number of people who feel uprooted from traditional religions and who yearn for a more experiential and Earth-connected spirituality. Modern Druidry, which seeks to rescue and revitalize the practices and philosophies of the ancient Druids, Celtic Neopaganism, which celebrates Celtic deities and festivals from a contemporary perspective, and other spiritual practices inspired by the Celtic tradition have gained popularity, offering a diverse range of approaches to experience Celtic spirituality in the modern world. This growing search demonstrates the relevance and attractiveness of Celtic spirituality in a world thirsty for meaning and connection with the transcendent.

Although the original Celtic languages have disappeared in much of continental Europe, as a testament to cultural resilience, some of them have survived and are being revitalized, like beacons of identity and tradition. Irish (Irish Gaelic), with its melodic sonority and rich history, Welsh, with its distinct pronunciation and vibrant literature, Scottish (Scottish Gaelic), spoken in the Highlands and islands of

Scotland, Breton, spoken in French Brittany, and Cornish, which underwent a remarkable revitalization process in English Cornwall, are examples of Celtic languages that resist time and globalization. The revitalization efforts of these languages, through education programs, cultural initiatives, and government support, demonstrate the value that Celtic communities attribute to their linguistic heritage as a central element of their cultural identity.

The festivals we celebrate today also carry echoes of ancient Celtic festivals, demonstrating the continuity of traditions and the adaptation of ancestral rituals to the modern context. Halloween, with its mysterious atmosphere and celebration of spirits, derives from Samhain, the Celtic festival that marked the end of summer and the beginning of winter, a liminal moment between worlds. Beltane, or May Day, with its bonfires and celebrations of fertility and life, has roots in the Celtic festival of Beltane, which celebrated the beginning of summer and the sacred union between the God and the Goddess. Yule, which influenced Christmas, with its celebration of the winter solstice and the rebirth of light, has origins in the Celtic festival of Yule, which marked the shortest day of the year and the promise of the return of light and life. These examples illustrate how modern festivals, although transformed by time and cultural influences, still preserve elements of ancient Celtic festivals, demonstrating the endurance of traditions and their ability to adapt and evolve.

Celtic values and customs, passed down from generation to generation, continue to be relevant and inspiring in our contemporary society. Hospitality, the art of receiving and warmly welcoming others, generosity, the predisposition to share and help, courage, the inner strength to face challenges, honor, integrity and loyalty to principles, deep respect for nature and awareness of its sacredness, and the importance of community, mutual support and solidarity, are Celtic values that resonate with universal human aspirations and that invite us to build a more just, compassionate, and harmonious society. These values, rooted in Celtic culture, offer an ethical guide for modern life, reminding us of the importance of authentic human relationships, the connection with nature, and the search for a deeper meaning in life.

Tourism, as a cultural industry, also contributes to the preservation and dissemination of the Celtic legacy. Imposing and mysterious archaeological sites, such as Stonehenge, with its enigmatic stone circles, Newgrange, with its ancestral corridor tomb, and other megalithic monuments scattered throughout Europe, attract thousands of tourists every year, from all over the world, fascinated by the history and culture of the ancient Celts. These places, charged with energy and mystery, awaken curiosity and imagination, inviting us to travel through time and connect with our ancestral roots. Cultural tourism around the Celtic legacy contributes to the local economy, promotes the preservation of heritage, and raises awareness of the importance of Celtic history and culture.

Tattoos, as a form of personal and artistic expression, have adopted Celtic designs with enthusiasm and creativity. The intricate Celtic knots, symbolic animals such as the deer, the boar, and the raven, and other Celtic symbols have become popular choices for tattoos, adorning the skin with meaning and aesthetic beauty. Celtic tattoos, in addition to their decorative value, can represent the connection with the Celtic heritage, the expression of values such as strength, courage, and spirituality, or simply the appreciation of Celtic aesthetics. The popularity of Celtic tattoos demonstrates how Celtic culture continues to inspire and influence contemporary trends, finding new forms of expression and adaptation in the modern world.

In an increasingly globalized, technological, and materialistic world, the Celtic tradition emerges as a beacon of ancestral wisdom, offering a valuable and necessary perspective to face the challenges of the 21st century. Its message resonates with our deepest needs, pointing the way to a fuller, more balanced, and meaningful life.

The reconnection with nature is an urgent imperative in the context of the environmental crisis we face. Celtic spirituality reminds us of the vital importance of honoring and protecting nature, of recognizing its intrinsic sacredness, of living in harmony with the cycles of life, and of understanding that we are an integral part of the web of life. At a time when the unrestrained exploitation of natural resources threatens the ecological balance of the planet, the Celtic tradition offers a model of a sustainable relationship with nature, based on respect, gratitude, and responsibility. Reconnecting with nature, following the Celtic example, can be a fundamental step towards building a greener and more harmonious future for all.

The appreciation of creativity is essential in a society that often prioritizes productivity and efficiency over artistic expression and the enjoyment of beauty. The Celtic tradition inspires us to cultivate our innate creativity, unleash our artistic potential, celebrate the beauty that surrounds us, and find joy and meaning in art, music, poetry, and other forms of creative expression. In a world increasingly focused on pragmatism and logic, the Celtic tradition reminds us of the importance of imagination, intuition, and the ability to dream and create. Valuing creativity, following the Celtic spirit, can enrich our lives, awaken our sensitivity, and make the world a more beautiful and inspiring place.

Strengthening community is crucial in an increasingly individualistic and fragmented world. The Celtic tradition reminds us of the importance of social bonds, cooperation, solidarity, and mutual support. At a time when social isolation and lack of human connection are growing problems, the Celtic tradition offers a model of community life, based on sharing, reciprocity, and a sense of belonging. Strengthening the community, inspired by Celtic values, can build support networks, promote social cohesion, and create a sense of belonging and security that is fundamental to individual and collective well-being.

The search for a deeper meaning in life is a fundamental human need, especially in an era when many people feel lost, disoriented, and without purpose.

Celtic spirituality offers a path of self-discovery, connection with the divine, and the search for a deeper meaning for existence. Through the exploration of nature, meditation, introspection, and the practice of meaningful rituals, the Celtic tradition can help us find answers to the great questions of life, discover our individual purpose, and live more authentically and aligned with our deepest values. The search for a deeper meaning, following the Celtic inspiration, can bring more clarity, direction, and fulfillment to our lives.

The rescue of ancestral wisdom is an act of respect for the past and recognition of its relevance to the present and the future. The Celtic tradition invites us to honor our ancestors, to learn from their wisdom accumulated over generations, and to rescue values and practices that can help us live more fully and meaningfully in the modern world. In a world that often despises the past and values only novelty and technology, the Celtic tradition reminds us that ancestral wisdom can be a valuable source of guidance and inspiration. Rescuing ancestral wisdom, following the Celtic example, can enrich our understanding of the world, strengthen our cultural identity, and offer solutions to contemporary challenges.

The preservation of cultural identity is of utmost importance, especially for the descendants of ancestral cultures such as the Celtic. Keeping the Celtic tradition alive is more than preserving the past, it is keeping the flame of cultural identity burning, transmitting values, practices, language, and stories from generation to generation. For descendants of Celts, the Celtic tradition represents a link with their roots, a sense of belonging, and a source of pride. Preserving cultural identity, following the Celtic example, is an act of cultural resistance, of valuing diversity and enriching human heritage.

The future of Celtic spirituality looks promising, as its message and values respond to many of the needs and anxieties of the contemporary world. Its emphasis on nature, community, creativity, spirituality, and ancestral wisdom offers a path to building a more balanced, just, sustainable, and harmonious world. The growing interest in Celtic culture and spirituality in recent decades indicates a trend that should continue to intensify. More and more people are looking for ways to reconnect with their roots, with nature and with the sacred, and the Celtic tradition offers a rich and inspiring path for this journey of search and self-discovery.

However, it is essential that this rescue of the Celtic tradition be done in a conscious, respectful, and responsible way. We must avoid cultural appropriation, which distorts and disrespects original cultures, the excessive romanticization of the past, which idealizes and simplifies complex realities, and the creation of reductive and caricatured stereotypes. It is essential to seek a deep and authentic knowledge of Celtic culture, learning from reliable sources, respecting different traditions and lineages, and adapting ancestral teachings to our contemporary reality with discernment and sensitivity. The future of Celtic spirituality depends on our ability to honor the past, to live the present with awareness, and to build a future in which the ancestral wisdom of the Celts can continue to inspire and guide humanity towards a path of light and harmony. May we be worthy of this valuable legacy, and may we use it with wisdom and responsibility to create a more beautiful, just, and magical world for all.

This is the end of the book "Celtic Rituals: A Practical and Spiritual Guide." I hope it has been an enriching and inspiring journey for you. May the ancestral wisdom of the Celts illuminate your path and strengthen your connection with nature, with the divine, and with your own essence. May Celtic magic always be present in your life!

Epilogue

The journey through the pages of this book was not just a trip to the past, but an invitation to the present - a call to awaken the ancestral spirituality that dwells within each of us. The Celts, with their deep connection to nature and their understanding of the cycles of life, left us a legacy that transcends time. They teach us that spirituality is not a rigid doctrine, but a continuous flow of learning, celebration, and transformation.

Each ritual described here, each symbol, each tradition rescues a long-dormant knowledge, waiting for those who have eyes to see and a heart to feel. Perhaps you have found, throughout these pages, an echo of something familiar, a subtle reminder that your soul has already walked this path before. This is because Celtic wisdom does not belong only to the past; it is timeless and continues to whisper in the wind, in the waters of the rivers, in the sunlight, and in the dance of the leaves as they fall in autumn.

Now, as you close this book, the inevitable question arises: what now? What to do with all this knowledge, this magic and this rescued connection? The answer is simple, but profound: to live. To live with the awareness that each dawn is a new cycle, each season brings its own teachings, and each breath is a prayer.

The Celts saw existence as a great dance, where the visible and the invisible are continuously intertwined. Celtic spirituality does not ask for grand temples, inflexible dogmas, or complex sacrifices. It only asks that we reconnect with the sacred that is already around us - in the earth beneath our feet, in the fire that warms our homes, in the water that purifies us, and in the air that inspires us.

The true teaching of this book is not only in the words that were read, but in what was felt. With each ritual practiced, with each connection established, you strengthen the bonds with your own essence and with the natural world. More than following instructions, it is about listening to intuition, for it is in it that true knowledge resides.

If there is one thing that the Celts taught us, it is that there is no definitive end - only cycles that renew themselves. The closing of this reading is, in fact, a new beginning. May the lessons absorbed here echo in your daily life, may the Wheel of the Year become more than a concept, and may the sacred rites gain space in your path.

May Celtic magic blossom in your life, and may the ancestors guide your steps with wisdom and protection. The legacy of the ancients continues to live in each of us, waiting to be remembered, celebrated, and honored.

May your journey be illuminated and may the gods and spirits of nature always accompany your steps.

www.ingramcontent.com/pod-product-compliance
Lightning Source LLC
LaVergne TN
LVHW040054080526
838202LV00045B/3623